ONE MOTHER

OF A

PORN

STAR

BOOK TWO OF FOUR

A TRUE LIFE SAGA OF ABUSE, VIOLENCE, AND ONE WOMAN'S STRUGGLE TO PROTECT THE CHILDREN SHE LOVES

NANCY TURNER

First Edition/Book Two of Four/2014
e-Book Publishing/Paperback

Cover Design by Derek Murphy

ISBN: 978-0692518045

ACKNOWLEDGMENTS

Dedicated To:

My Al-Anon Sponsor, Fred D.
Without him, I would not have found Betty T.

To my Son's AA Sponsor, Bradley D.
For being the light that guided my son to sobriety.

To my Angels
Had they not spoken to me and protected my life,
I would not be here to tell my story.

To God
For sending Bertie Catchings and Bonnae M. into my life
to give me hope for a better future.

TABLE OF CONTENTS

1

≈

The Family Splinters

My phone rang. "Debbie, I got married last week to a nice lady with two young children."

Instantly, my heart stopped when I heard Bart's voice. Here I sit, left in the wake of this asshole's total destruction of my life and my family, and he wants to call and rub salt in my wounds. He destroyed everything I valued in life; a loving, faithful husband who would help me raise my two children. Everyone, I mean everyone, thought we had The Perfect Marriage.

"How old are her children, Bart?"

"Her daughter's seven and the boy's nine."

"Is that a good idea?"

"What does that mean?"

"It means I'm concerned about her children, after what happened to my kids during our marriage."

"Nothing will happen to them. I thought you'd be happy for me. I've had a lot of time to think. I'm a changed man. Wait and see." He hung up. *My mind revisited that God awful pain one more time.* Then, I said a silent prayer for that unsuspecting family.

✳ ✳ ✳

Three months later, I received a five a.m. phone call from an operator. "Will you accept a collect call from Stacy Malone?"

"Yes, I will."

The only time Stacy phones me in the middle of the night is when he's in some kind of trouble.

"Mom, I'm scared. It's three a.m." *He sounds out of breath.*

"I walked to a train station and zigzagged past the San Francisco Mint. I noticed drops of blood every six feet. Soon, the drops became a steady trail. Street lights guided my nervous feet into Dubuque Park. The ominous trail of blood ended at a nearby phone booth. I peered inside and panic ripped through me. A pool of blood was all over the booth floor. I shouted, 'Oh, God!' I looked around to see if the victim was nearby and needed help. No one was there. I raced to the corner bus stop. To my relief, the airport bus will arrive in five minutes. I'm flying home tonight."

"Do you have enough money for airfare?"

"Dad mailed me his credit card."

"Thank God you're coming home, before something terrible happens to you!"

✵ ✵ ✵

That was the last page of Book One. Finally, my plane landed in Paris, France. I caught a taxi to Hotel Bedford located in the center of Paris. After I checked into the hotel, I turned to go to the elevator. I ran into little Candice from my flight to Paris and met her mother. We had a nice chat. I wished them well in court and then rode the elevator upstairs.

After I changed clothes, I went downstairs to Restaurant Le Victoria just off the lobby of Hotel Bedford and was seated by the maître d'hôtel. I ordered my food and noticed a nice looking gentleman at a nearby table. His attire was a bit flamboyant; a white suit, red tie, and red handkerchief. I was unsure if his bleached blond hair was real. He wore lots of gold jewelry.

As I ate my meal, I glanced at him. I noticed he was reading Book Two of Debbie Austin's journey. I stood up and approached him. "Sir, where did you purchase that book? I just read Book One. I didn't think Book Two was released yet."

He smiled and replied in a strong British accent. "Would you like to join me?"

"Yes, I would like that." The maître d'hôtel quickly moved my meal to the stranger's table, and I sat down.

"I am a Book Reviewer by trade. That is how I obtained an unpublished copy of her book. It is due for release in one month."

"Tell me your impression of Debbie Austin's journey."

"Honestly, I could not have survived even three of the things that poor woman has gone through thus far. I'm amazed by her discipline of handling problems, a job, a family and not *going crazy*."

I nodded. "She's already lived through much more than most people do in one lifetime, and there's more to come."

His eyes twinkled. "I tell you what I will do. After I finish this book, I will have it sent to your room."

"That would be perfect. I can read it when I fly back to New York next week. I'm in Room 218. Thank you!"

He stood up, squeezed my hand and left. I was so excited that I barely slept all night.

✻ ✻ ✻

The next morning, I went sightseeing in Paris for the first time. The Eiffel Tower and The Louvre were on day one. The Arc de Triomphe and Notre-Dame de Paris filled up day two. On my last day, I shopped at Boulevard Haussmann and purchased several beautiful pictures and statues there.

Early on the fourth day, I packed my bags for my return flight to New York. Someone knocked on my door. "Who is it?"

"I'm the bellhop with a package." I opened the door, accepted it and tipped him. Now to get to the airport, board my plane and read Book Two of Debbie Austin's journey.

First, I want one last look out my window at Paris. In hours, my New York flight lifted off, and I opened Book Two.

✳ ✳ ✳

A gay friend of Stacy's named Tom Hamm picked him up at the nearby airport and dropped him off at home the next day. When he entered the front door, I hurried to give him a big hug. "I'm so glad you're home in one piece, honey."

He carried his tattered bag into the den and went to the fridge to get a soda pop. "Have I missed anything since I've been gone?"

"Yes, you're officially an uncle again. Crystal and Steve welcomed little Wayne Jordan Simmons a week after you left. They also moved into a new home. I gave them my couch and bought a new one."

Stacy grinned. "Does Wayne look like Steve or Crystal?"

"He looks more like Steve's side of the family. He has big, greenish eyes and a nice head of auburn hair."

"Maybe I'll drive over in a few of days and surprise her."

"I'm sure she'd like that. Where are you planning to live, now that you're back? You can't keep a job, and I just now got your room put back together after you trashed it."

"So?"

"So, where can I put you?"

"I can sleep on the back porch."

"Don't be silly, but maybe..."

"Maybe what?"

"Yeah, maybe you could make a room out in the garage."

"There's no heat in the winter or air in the summer."

"I can fix that, but there will be some conditions."

"Like what?"

"Like, agree you'll finish high school this fall."

"Okay. What else?"

"Keep a day-rate sheet."

"What's that?"

"Write what you did each day; how you felt about your day. And rate it on a scale of one to ten; ten being the best!"

"That's no problem."

"Also, you will read a Bible verse daily and note which verse you read on your sheet."

"Anything else?"

"Yes, one more thing."

"Which is what?"

"Get into treatment."

"Treatment?"

"Correct, or consider going to AA."

"My problem *isn't that I'm an alcoholic*, it's that I'm gay."

"If that's the case, I saw a news story on TV. There's a new church in town called *AIM; Alternative Identification Ministries*. They help gays go straight."

"I'll have to think about that one." Stacy opened his bag and pulled out something for me. It was a unicorn wind chime. "I know how much you like unicorns."

I beamed. "I love it! I'll hang it in the corner by the dining table."

Stacy went to the garage thru the pantry and quickly returned. "It looks like we need to have a garage sale, before I can make an apartment out of our garage."

"Fine, but our deal still includes AA or that AIM group."

"Okay, okay, but first, let me get my room fixed up."

"We'll start tomorrow."

I grabbed my camera, followed Stacy thru the pantry and down the steps into our garage. "I want some before-and-after pictures of your new room." I snapped a *before picture*. It showed stacks of clothes, boxes and lots of disarray and many scattered items everywhere.

✳ ✳ ✳

Two days later, I took an *after picture*. It showed a spacious, well-arranged apartment complete with throw rugs, two couches, end tables, a TV, stereo, lamps, my pool table, a Sebring juke box I won and a regular-sized bed.

By the weekend, our garage sale was in full swing. We sold off many unwanted items from the garage. Those that didn't sell were given to Goodwill later that day.

When Stacy saw the pictures of his new room, he decided to add movie posters and his beer can collection along the walls. As a finishing touch, I bought rolls of black plastic. He used it to lower the high garage ceiling, and he hung two round Chinese paper lamps in the center. When he had it finished, I was astonished. "Wow, this is spacious enough to be a New York Flat."

✳ ✳ ✳

On Saturday, Stacy left to surprise Crystal. I went to see a movie; *Good Morning, Vietnam*. When I returned home, I knocked on Stacy's door. "Are you asleep?" He didn't answer, so I opened the door. His light was off.

"I'm awake."

I walked down the steps and approached his bed. "Why are you in the dark?"

"It's my sister."

"What about her?"

"I rang their doorbell. She stepped outside and closed their door. 'Stacy, I prefer that you not come by here anymore because of my kids.' "

"What are you talking about?"

"You know, you're gay, and I have little boys and..."

I cut her off. "I'm gay. I'm not a pedophile."

She shrugged and went back inside their home, so I left.

"You're her brother. She owes you an apology."

Before I got a chance to see Crystal and talk to her about how she treated her brother, I received a phone call from Steve five days later. *I could tell he was extremely upset by his heavy breathing.* "Debbie, Crystal just left me with Daniel and Wayne. She's gone for good."

"This won't do. Mother's don't leave their children. I didn't leave my kids, and Crystal isn't going to leave hers."

"She said that she wasn't coming back."

"Oh yes she will. I'll talk to her." I hung up the phone in shock, drove to Steve's home and rang the doorbell. He let me inside. Daniel was playing with some cars on the floor. Steve was feeding Wayne his bottle of baby formula. "Steve, any idea where Crystal went?"

He fought back tears. "No, I don't. I want her back. I love her. We need her at home."

"I'm going to call some of her friends to see if anyone has heard from her. I'll keep in touch."

"Can I call you?"

"Of course. I'm here for you any time day-or-night."

It was hard to leave Steve sitting there with a broken heart and two little angels. Daniel isn't even his child, but he loves him as if he were. Wayne is almost seven-months-old. *Dear God, Crystal has lost her mind. I swear I just don't know my daughter anymore.*

✳ ✳ ✳

I spent the next two days calling Crystal's friends. No luck. Then, my phone rang.

"Mom, I guess you've heard that I left Steve."

"Yep, and you also left your children behind. Mothers don't leave their kids! You need to go back home right now and..."

"I made up my mind. I'm not going back."

"You are if I have anything to say about it."

"Well, you don't! This is my life. I don't answer to you anymore."

"Wrong! You deserted my grandsons. Don't have kids if you don't want them. You had them. That means they are *your responsibility.* Poor Steve is devastated. He loves you and wants you back home."

"I just rented an apartment and landed a job at a radio station."

"Don't come crying to me when you fall on your face."

"I won't. I can take care of myself." She slammed the phone in my ear. I circled February 20, 1987, on my calendar and wrote "Crystal left Steve and her kids." *Instantly, shame overwhelmed me. How could any child of mine think so little of her own children?*

I knew Stacy should be home from school, so I turned to find him when the phone rang.

A familiar, angry voice erupted through the receiver. "You fucking bitch! Why the fucking hell did you phone my new wife and tell her all that shit about Crystal?" *Bart had only screamed at me like that during our divorce. Once was the day he was served with Incest Charges on Crystal. His unexpected tone hit me like a bucket of ice water. Maybe I should hang up. Then, an old sadness walked into my heart once again.*

"I don't know what you're talking about, Bart. I don't have your phone number. I would *not* call and tell her about Crystal."

"It had to be you. Otherwise, how the fuck did she find out all that shit? She's divorcing my ass."

"I'm sorry to hear that, but I assure you I had nothing to do with her finding out about Crystal."

He slammed the phone in my ear. *And to think, I was crazy in love with this man for eleven years. Part of me still longs for those days when we were so in love. I can't explain it, but my heart still yearns for that sweet, loving man I thought I knew. He was my dream husband, the love of my life. I owe this ugly bastard side of him zero respect. In fact, he's damn lucky I didn't know his bastard side on that cold March morning, or I might have plastered his brains across our mirrored headboard. I let it go and returned to reality.*

✳ ✳ ✳

I knocked on Stacy's garage door. He was resting on his bed, reading a *Black Sabbath* magazine, and listening to a Guns N' Roses song, "Welcome to the Jungle."

"I'd like to see your day-rate sheet and which Bible verses you've read so far." When he showed them to me, I was pleased. "That's great, honey. Now when are you going to visit an AA meeting or AIM? You made a commitment to me, and I expect you to keep it."

"Mother, I'm not an alcoholic like Dad. My only problem is that I'm gay and need help to *change*. If this AIM group has found a way to do that, I'll try it."

"Good, let me call and see when you can start." I smiled all the way to the telephone, dialed and spoke with a friendly man. "We will be starting a new group on Monday at eight a.m."

"I'll be there with my son. Thank you."

On Monday, I drove Stacy across town, parked, and went inside with him. We met Minister Craig. He seemed nice, honest and sincerely persuasive. "Stacy, with my guidance, I know that our program can change you from being gay." With that, he walked Stacy down the wide hallway. I turned and left. *I can only hope.*

For about three weeks, things seemed to go fine, until the last week. Stacy didn't get up that Monday morning. I opened his garage door. "Stacy, you're going to be late."

He grumbled. "I'm not going there anymore."

"Why is that?" I approached his bed.

"I don't like that place. That's why."

"What happened?"

"Minister Craig forcefully came on to me. I had to fight him off. He must be gay!"

I almost choked. "What a fraud!"

✻ ✻ ✻

My curiosity finally got the best of me a month later, after Stacy returned home from visiting with old friends. He plopped on the den couch beside me. "Honey, I'd like to hear more about your time in San Francisco." *It is said that we must be careful what we ask for.* Stacy related the following story to me.

✻ ✻ ✻

I approached Simon, after I deplaned in San Francisco. He posed and spoke in his deepest, sexy voice.

"What kept you so long, *whore?*"

Then, he brushed past me and put his hands on his skinny hips. His eyes pranced up-and-down my attire.

"Well, well, look at you, Mr. G.Q.! Did the *Gentleman's Quarterly* recommend those rags or did you steal them?"

"Stop it! I'm dressed like this for travel. This trip isn't a Punk Rock event."

He quickly changed the subject.

"Hey Man, you'll like Mom's house; yellow-and-white, 1890's three-story look, hardwood floors, no air conditioning, but it sits on the downside of a steep hill facing San Francisco Bay."

"And earthquakes?"

"We get tremors sometimes, but not to worry. I'll settle you in at Mom's house tomorrow. Tonight, you'll stay with me."

As I followed Simon to find his friend's old van buried in the sprawling parking lot, I silently questioned myself. *What have I done?* Just as quickly, I thought, *Oh, what the hell!* The moment we turned the corner and drove toward Simon's house, deja' vu hit me. I had seen this exact scene before, possibly in a dream. He lived in an old Victorian-style home in the Haight-Asbury District. Californians called them *Flats.* He parked and led me up a graduated stairway into a stylish, old house. Inside, I saw hardwood floors, old fixtures, small rooms and an antique-looking kitchen, exactly as I had envisioned. Strangely, I knew which room I'd be sleeping in and walked straight to the door. Simon squinted at me, as his wide brow slowly rose.

"Gee Stacy, been here before?"

I knew when he shoved the wooden door open that I'd see a strange-looking bed sitting high upon milk crates, with a wide-edged bay window looking toward the north and Punk Rock posters thumbtacked to his walls. My accuracy didn't surprise me. For a short while, we talked about old times, but I kept staring at his strange drug posters on the wall. Shortly, I noticed a charcoal self-portrait he'd done that showed track marks on both of his arms. Simon talked extensively about himself.

"Sophie moved to San Francisco, after I saw her dance on New Year's Eve. Remember our double date? Even though I'm only eighteen and she's twenty-five, we have a lot in common, baby."

I fell asleep on his bed, while he was talking. I never knew when he slipped across his hall to sleep with his girlfriend, Sophie. I woke up early the next morning. Terror slapped me in the face. Pure panic churned through my mind. *Oh, God. I'm seventeen-hundred-miles away from home. Simon is strangely different. I sense a complete change in him. He must be deep into drugs. I'm so screwed.* Then, Simon suddenly appeared in the doorway.

"So Stacy, just what brought you to me?"

Sarcastic rudeness oozed from each of his words. I sprung upright in his strange bed, as if I'd been shot. I felt uncomfortable and confused about my old friend's shocking switch of attitude.

"Well, Simon, I needed a change and wanted to see how life in San Francisco would compare to home."

"How trite. *You needed me for a change...*"

My eyes rolled down the top of the bed and off to the right. My mind frantically searched for any sign of sanity inside the room. Suddenly, a twenty-something, red-headed Punk Rocker came barging in the room. Simon rolled his eyes toward the ceiling.

"Stacy, meet my *real Punk Rock friend, Johnny.*"

2

≈

Surprise, Surprise, Surprise

I was sitting on the bed, when Johnny flopped down beside me and gushed. "Oh, Simon, I have to show you what I found today. I'm so excited!" He opened a black leather pouch slung over his left shoulder and removed a black Colt .45 revolver. My eyes widened.

"I bought it for just ten dollars. *It's so me!*" He placed the loaded gun right beside me. A second wave of terror shot through me. *What are they into? Why the excitement about this gun? When is the next plane back home?* Sadly, my alcoholic pride kept me there.

At ten a.m., Simon's sister, Angel, arrived and offered to escort me to her mother's house. During the trip, I gripped Bill's old suitcase he gave me extra tight. It contained all my worldly possessions. On the way, we passed many communities; the rich, middle-class, Punk Rockers, gays, druggies and street people. Simon's mother, Linda, reminded me of a tall version of Lucille Ball in a hippie wardrobe. She led me down some stairs.

"I can only offer you a single bed, chest-of-drawers and a slightly-worn chair. Set up a room down here any way you want."

"That will be great!"

My night was restless. The next morning, I constructed a room using wire that I crisscrossed and then draped blankets and sheets over it to form walls. That afternoon, Linda came down to see my room. "Stacy, have dinner with us at six p.m. Oh, by the way, this room is *clever.*"

At supper, I felt welcome. Strangely enough, we each filled a void for the other. I needed a family, and Linda needed a son. I had an instant family.

✳ ✳ ✳

Soon, I was hired as a waiter at the new *Margaritaville* on Union Street. Three weeks passed before Simon surfaced and invited me to visit his house again. As I walked to Linda's front door, she surprised me.

"Stacy, I hope you'll earn part of your keep by talking to Simon about *things.*"

"Things? What things?"

"Oh, it's just his way of life. You were always his role-model in high school."

"I was?"

"Yes. To him, *you were it.*"

"I never knew."

That night, I rode the BART to Simon's house. He appeared to be on a drug high, as he led me into his room. I noticed he had placed a high school picture of me beside his bed and painted the wooden crates under his bed fire-engine red. *How strange!* Then, he ignored me for an hour to label his records.

"Well Stacy, how do you like the big SF?"

"It has a lot to offer."

"What would you change about it?"

"I'd have my family live here, too."

"Need a security blanket?"

"No. I miss seeing them."

"Grow up!"

"Listen, this isn't high school. I'm not taking your crap!"

"Yes, you will. It is I who now has the upper hand."

✻ ✻ ✻

I smiled at Stacy. "Honey, I want to hear the rest of your story later, but I need to talk to you about something else. I'd like to take you to a free clinic to get you tested for AIDS. They will also give you guidance for *Safe Sex*. With so many young men dying of AIDS right now, I want to know you aren't going to be one of them."

"Okay, Mom, if that will make you feel better."

"It will. I don't want anything happening to you."

✻ ✻ ✻

The next morning, we entered a free clinic. A female nurse took Stacy into a lab area and tested his blood for AIDS. While we waited on the results, a male nurse took him into a room, showed him a short film on *Safe Sex,* gave him some condoms to use and answered every question he had. Afterward, we waited for his test results. Finally, a female nurse approached. "Good news, Stacy is healthy."

"Oh, thank God!" We left their office. *A huge worry was just lifted off my shoulders.*

When we arrived at home, Stacy headed to the front door. "I'm going to have lunch with my Drama Club friend, Tom."

"Sounds good. I need to get ready for work."

I watched Stacy drive away through our front bay window, took a shower, dressed, and then, I heard the front doorbell ring. I opened the door and there stood Crystal. She hurried inside all aglow, sat on one of my barstools and oozed, "Guess who I just saw today?"

"Steve and your children?"

"No, Mother. I ran into Darren, Bart's son. We had lunch. He looks great! He's finally taller than me and has a moustache. We're going to have lunch again in two weeks."

"Is he married?"

"He's divorced, like me."

"You aren't divorced. You just moved out on your family."

"I don't want to talk about it."

"Well, I do."

"Not today. I'm happy, and that's all that matters." Crystal hopped off the barstool, left in a huff and drove away in her car.

I closed the front door and heard the knob turn two minutes later. Stacy walked into the den. "Was that my sister who didn't want me in her home anymore?"

"It sure was. She ran into Darren, after all these years. He was eight-years-old the day Bart suddenly took him home, after he knocked you off our slide."

"Those rose bushes did a bad number on me."

"That's true. You know, summer school starts in three months. How about you go visit Principal Stinson and find out if he will allow you to return to high school?"

"I guess, but what if he won't allow it?"

"He'll get a visit from me."

✳ ✳ ✳

A week later, I sat beside Stacy on our den couch. "I'm ready to hear more of your story about Simon and San Francisco." Stacy nodded and picked up where he had left off.

✳ ✳ ✳

Simon soon brought up our *Rocky Horror* gang and Patty.

"Those days in Drama Club with Patty and the cast were the best of days."

"Simon, do you realize that Patty's been dead a year and two months?"

"You loved her terribly."

"Yes, terribly."

"Stacy, are you gay?"

"Yeah."

Simon began twisting weird knots in a rope. "Why didn't you let me know?"

"Why should I?"

"Dumb prick. I was in love with you!"

"No way! It was just boyhood sex. We were so young. I was never in love with you."

"You were the first guy I ever had feelings for and..."

"Why did you beg me to come here and then ignore me?"

"To see my role model one more time." *A sick feeling crawled inside my body. I feel like Dr. Frankenstein.*

Simon gave me a demonic grin. "I've got something wonderful to show you. It's *Pandora's Box!*"

He slid a large matchbox from beneath his tall bed frame, lit a large candle, sat on his funky bed, crossed his legs and patted the mattress for me to sit beside him. My eyes weren't prepared for the contents of *Pandora's Box*. When he opened it, I saw needles, syringes, cotton balls, money, a scale, baggies and a small box filled with drugs staring back at me. *I'll be lucky to get out of here alive! Although curious, I can't understand why anyone would actually shoot-up.*

I watched Simon carefully carry his matchbox with both hands and sit it in the windowsill. Next, he turned on a gruesome record and returned to his windowsill perch. He put some speed in a tablespoon, added a touch of water and held the spoon over a candle flame. The heat broke the crystals into liquid form. After it cooled, he took a cotton ball and ceremoniously dropped it into the spoon. If I hadn't known better, I'd swear that I was observing a medical doctor at work. He picked up a syringe and loaded it by sticking the needle into the cotton ball and drawing out the drug until the cotton ball went white. Rays of sunlight trickled thru the window behind him and formed a slim silhouette that resembled *The Grim Reaper.*

I backed toward the door and stammered, "Well, Simon, I better go."

He held out his hand and beckoned, "Give me your arm. This is the greatest drug there is!"

"No, it's nothing I want to do right now. Simon, I've snorted coke, crystal and smoked marijuana, but I'm not into that hard stuff!"

"Fine! Then, I'll do it!"

I watched him tie a band around his skinny left arm. I grew ill over his sickening desperation, *as it worked him like a newborn maggot.* Finally, he pulled the needle out of his arm, dropped his pants, rubbed alcohol on his pale white, right hip cheek with a cotton ball and slammed the needle deep into his skin. I heard his soft whimper ripple through the air, as he leaned back against the window frame. Curiosity pulled me toward him for a closer look. His wild, blue eyes flickered in the pre-dawn light. His deep voice moaned.

"Oh! Wow! What a far-out high!"

Peer pressure lurked in the shadows, but I had no intention of *shooting-up.* Instead, I snorted a line of crystal, to somewhat oblige Simon's hospitality. As dawn arrived, I realized we'd spent the night listening to music, talking crazy and doing drugs. Suddenly, Simon stood up, stumbled to his synthesizer and began singing eerie songs into his floor microphone that matched his strange mood. I was shocked when he shot up again, so I pretended to snort more crystal. Actually, I slipped it into my shoe instead. Time vanished quickly that morning. When mid-afternoon arrived, he dove across his tall bed and announced, "I need some time alone."

✳ ✳ ✳

I interrupted Stacy. "No more. That's all I want to know."

✳ ✳ ✳

In weeks, Jay and I began to spend more time together. He was on his best behavior. Then, he started calling me late at night with *dirty phone sex talk. Clearly, he was masturbating while he was talking to me. It was a new experience for me. He was ultra-proud of his excessive endowment. I must admit, it was true.*

Jay finally talked me into spending the night at his apartment. Without a doubt, he was totally fascinating in bed. He warmed a soft cloth, placed it over my eyes and proceeded to gently kiss my body from head-to-toe. He totally took my breath away in the process.

It was about the same time when my boss, Archie, decided to retire. The company brought in a new boss from Los Angeles. He approached me. "Hi, I'm Ivan Stone. I am replacing Archie tomorrow." Ivan had gray hair, wore glasses and a nice smile. At first, he seemed nice enough. However, it didn't take long for him to change. *Working for Ivan was one of the worst times I ever endured with a boss. Needless to say, we didn't hit it off.*

And Jay soon decided he wanted to marry me again. This time, he used flowers to convince me and sent gorgeous flowers to my work. I had nowhere to put them, except on a table beside my work station. Ivan approached me. "What's the special occasion?"

"My boyfriend sent them."

"They're pretty."

Several co-workers passed by and commented on my flowers. I took them home after work and put them on my kitchen table.

The next week, Jay sent me a dozen red roses with a card that read, "Will you marry me, baby?"

Ivan stormed toward me. "Tell your boyfriend to *stop* sending you flowers at work."

That night, I phoned Jay. "My boss doesn't want me to get flowers at work again."

"He's not my boss. I will send my darlin' flowers if I want."

The next afternoon, more flowers arrived for me. Ivan made a beeline to my work station. "I thought I told you to stop getting flowers here?"

"I asked him to stop sending them. I can't control what he does."

Ivan snarled, "Put them on the floor!"

"Okay! Okay!" I placed my huge vase of red roses on the floor. People could still see them there and several asked me why they were on the floor.

Honestly, Ivan is the cruelest boss I ever endured. I finally convinced Jay to stop sending me flowers at work, but after that incident, Ivan clearly had it in for me. He began to harass me about my work, even though I was an excellent employee. It was a miserable time in my life. *It felt like I was working for Ivan the Terrible!*

✳ ✳ ✳

Principal Stinson allowed Stacy to return to high school with a warning. "This is your second and last time to return. Leave again, and you can't come back."

Two weeks passed, when Mother phoned. "I want to take you and Crystal to lunch. I'm driving there tomorrow." *Oh, this should get interesting quick, when Mother leans the truth about Crystal leaving Steve and the kids.*

"I haven't heard from her lately, Mother."

"Why not?"

"I'll tell you tomorrow." I hung up and phoned Steve. "Hi, do you have Crystal's phone number yet?"

He gave me her work number, so I called her. "Crystal, how did your second meeting with Darren go?"

There was a long pause. "He stood me up." *I hope Darren isn't going to follow Bart's example in life.*

"Mother will be here tomorrow. She wants to see you."

"Okay, but she better not lecture me."

"We'll meet you at Antonio's at noon tomorrow."

Crystal snapped. "I guess so." *Damn, not only is she mad at me, it sounds like she wants a Battle Royal with Mother.*

The next day, Mother arrived at 11:30 a.m. She admired my unicorn wind chime that Stacy gave me, while I phoned Crystal at work. "Hi, Mother's here. We're on our way."

"Okay. I may be a few minutes late. I'm real busy."

We arrived before Crystal and waited out front on a bench. She showed up ten minutes later. I noticed she had gained a little weight. We went inside and were seated by the hostess.

Mother turned to Crystal. "Why did you leave your family?"

"Who told you that?"

"I had a dream about it. Every time your mom or you were expecting, I also dreamed about it before I heard the news."

"I'm not going home. I'm dating a guy where I work."

Mother glared at her. "Dating? You're married. You have a great husband and two children. Don't mess up your life."

"It isn't messed up. I'm very happy. *I don't love Steve.*"

"Crystal, he calls me day-and-night. Steve is distraught. He still loves you."

Her face turned red. "I'm not going back. I like my life now."

Our food arrived, we ate and said our goodbye's outside the restaurant. Crystal rushed away to her car.

Mother looked at me. "Well, that didn't go very well."

"She's making a huge mistake, but what can I do about it?" *Then, a picture of Bart pretending to spank Crystal popped into my head. I guess that's what phony discipline gets you; one selfish child turned adult.*

✳ ✳ ✳

The next afternoon, Stacy entered the den and sat on the couch. I was reading the paper. "Guess where I went yesterday."

"To a movie?"

"Crystal called and invited me over to see her apartment."

"How was it?"

"It was okay. She was nice to me, but I didn't see any sign of a male living in her apartment."

"Good! She's married and has two children who need her. Did she mention the guy that she told me she's already dating?"

"No, she didn't."

Stacy went to his garage room, so I called Steve. "Hi, how are you and my little grandkids doing today?"

"We're lonesome. We miss Crystal and..." Steve choked up.

"I feel so helpless. Even mother can't get through to her."

"That's why I keep praying that she'll come back to us." *That makes three of us praying that she will return to her family.*

✳ ✳ ✳

The following week, I went into Stacy's garage room looking for something, glanced under the pool table and spotted a bedroll, pillow, radio, flashlight and some food. I realized someone was living there. Later, I confronted Stacy in his garage room. "I don't know who's living under our pool table, but they'll have to go."

"Yes, Ma'am," Stacy snapped indignantly.

"No more friends in the house until further notice."

He nodded. I turned and left his garage room.

Two weeks later, I walked into the garage after returning from a date and flipped on Stacy's light. "Stacy, I..." My words skidded to a halt in mid-sentence. I saw two nude bodies wrapped in a full embrace under Stacy's sheets. He sat up in bed and tried to shield his visitor's nude body from view.

"Tell him to get out of here right now!" I slammed his door with a vengeance. I soon heard the side garage door slam shut. I entered Stacy's garage room after he left and read his daily-rate sheets. His notes were darker in tone. His daily Bible verses had moved into Revelations and the damnation-type verses. Words of depression and hopelessness swarmed through his writings. Then, I read his most recent entry.

"I feel total rejection from all sides. My self-esteem has been swallowed up, because of my gay lifestyle. I doubt Mom will ever understand that I didn't choose to be gay any more than she chose to be a female. I know I'm stretching myself too far and in too many places, especially with Mom." *If Stacy only knew, I've had many gay friends at work over the years, but when it's your child, it takes time to adjust to that fact as a reality.*

✳ ✳ ✳

A month later, my phone rang as I was leaving for work. "Mom, I'm pregnant, and I'm going to get an abortion."

Crystal wants to abort a child, because it's inconvenient for her? I went through Bloody Hell to protect her and myself from being killed by her frigging horrible dad! Otherwise, both of us would not be alive today and neither would her two children.

"No way in hell do I agree with this! We don't abort our babies!"

"I'm getting an abortion, and you can't stop me!"

"Over my dead body! I didn't abort you, and you aren't going to abort this baby!"

"I will if I want to!"

"And I will do everything in my power to stop you."

"I hate you, bitch!" She slammed the phone in my ear.

I heard nothing from Crystal for weeks.

About noon on Monday, August 24, 1987, my phone finally rang. "Mom, I need your help." *She hates me one day and pleads for my help weeks later.*

"You need my help to do what?"

"I'm definitely getting an abortion. I've already made an appointment. I just need someone to drive me home."

"You called the wrong person."

"What am I going to do?"

"Cancel your abortion appointment!"

3

≈

When Will This Madness End

"This abortion is going to happen, whether you like it or not."

I paused in thought for a long time. *Crystal just doesn't understand. If I had aborted her, we wouldn't be having this conversation today.*

"It's only because you are my daughter and I love you, that I would *ever* agree to drive you home. Understand, I will *never* approve of what you're doing. You have to live with your decision, not me."

"Then, will you drive me home afterward?"

"I guess, but it's under protest." I hung up.

Immediately, I phoned Steve. "I just heard from Crystal."

"How is she doing?"

"She's pregnant and plans to abort her baby. I told her I would stop her anyway I could. Will you help me stop her?"

"It can't be my child. It's been way too long since we were together."

"I know. She's adamant that she's going through with it."

Steve's voice grew sad. "I haven't even heard from her in weeks, not even to ask about her own children, and now she wants to abort a baby?" *I'm not sure whose desperation is the greatest right now, mine or Steve's. Why must an innocent baby die, just because Crystal made a mistake?*

"I'm desperate, Steve. I can't accept her decision to go through with this abortion. Please talk some sense into her!"

Steve was silent for a moment. "I will call her right now."

✷ ✷ ✷

Two days later, my phone rang after I woke up. "Debbie, I owe you an apology." *Man, this is a first. Bart never apologizes for anything. I want him to totally own his hate-filled rant from the other day.*

"What are you talking about, Bart?"

"I finally discovered how my new wife learned about Crystal and then filed for divorce. It wasn't you after all."

"That's exactly what I told you, but you were too busy cussing me out to hear what I was saying."

"She found that tape you secretly made and gave to the police to get me indicted."

"And, how did *you* get it? I have it and..."

"Well, I..."

"You rat! You must have stolen it from me while you were living here briefly, and Rhonda was busy trashing every job you could find. Damn you! I had it well hidden in my closet. You *totally* deserve what happened to you. I don't blame her one bit for leaving you. I wish I had listened to your ex-wife. I could have spared my family all of this grief you've caused us."

"I just wanted you to know. At least, I'm admitting it. Yes, I took it the day I came back to get my tools. Stacy let me in."

"You know, I should have known better than to get involved with someone who burglarized the Red Rock National Bank. And then, you went next door to visit with the local police. Plus, you almost pulled it off, until you took your good friend, Jeff, to Juarez with you to sell some guns."

"Yes, I did, and I could have probably avoided prison time, if I hadn't told him about that bank burglary. He got so drunk at the hotel bar that night that he blabbed it. One of those Chicanos must have heard him and turned us in for a reward."

"It sounds to me like you wanted to get caught."

"Maybe I did. The next morning, we loaded all of my guns into my car and heard, 'Freeze, Federal Agents!' For a moment that day, I paused and wondered. *Is this worth dying for?*"

"I guess it wasn't."

"Good old Jeff. *He fried me good!* He got off with a minor fine and probation for turning State's evidence on me. I served three concurrent sentences and did one year of hard time."

I closed my eyes. *I feel like I've served a hell of a lot more time than that, because I married your sorry ass.*

"Bart, I hope you've learned your lesson on all counts. Try to stay out of trouble."

"Yes, Ma'am." He hung up.

I ate a small breakfast and got ready for work. Three hours later, I opened the front door to leave when my phone rang.

"Debbie, Crystal has agreed to cancel her abortion and move back home."

"Thank God! How did you manage to convince her?"

"I told her, 'I want the baby whether you do or not. Just have the baby and give it to me.' She decided to move back home." After I hung up the phone, tears of joy streamed down my cheeks. *That little baby now has a chance to have a future and a life of his own.*

✸ ✸ ✸

Stacy began to stay out later and later each night, usually with his gay friends, Tom or Donny. *At least there's no one living underneath our pool table anymore.*

One day, I wandered into Stacy's garage room to empty his trash can, when something odd caught my eye. A tall object was leaning against the garage wall with a blanket over it. I dropped my trash bag and uncovered it. *Dear God, it's a huge city sign and probably a misdemeanor.*

Stacy's Garage Room

✳ ✳ ✳

I woke Stacy up the next morning. "What in the world were you thinking?"

"Huh? What do you mean?"

I pointed at the uncovered historical sign from a famous, local park. "Obviously, you stole that sign. I want you to return it. I don't want it in my home."

"If I return it, I could get arrested."

"That's not my problem. That's your problem." *Even so, that sign remained in my garage for the longest time.*

It was about a month before I began to realize the true significance of that historical sign from Red Rock River Park. I was watching the local news on TV. Local police were called to arrest five carloads of teenagers who were either drunk, on drugs, or passed out at that park. *I can only hope that Stacy isn't in one of those cars.*

✳ ✳ ✳

Labor Day, September 5, 1987, was approaching. Steve phoned me. "I'm taking Crystal to see fireworks on Labor Day at the Red Rock Stadium. I'd like for you to join us." *I have no idea what to expect from Crystal.*

"Okay, I'd like that. I'll meet you all at the front gate."

Two nights later, I drove across downtown and found Crystal and Steve waiting for me beside the main gate. Steve was holding little Wayne. Crystal uttered *not one word to me.* Steve and I talked, as we walked inside the stadium and found good seats.

Once we were seated, I took a picture of the three of them. *If looks could kill, I would have instantly keeled over dead from the rays of pure hatred shooting from my daughter's eyes at me.* Her arms were folded and an ugly, hateful scowl covered her angry face. *Dear God. She's pissed at me but good, probably because I phoned Steve. I'm going to ignore her and her childish temper tantrum.* Steve and I talked across her. She remained sullen the whole evening! Plus, she virtually ignored little Wayne.

✳ ✳ ✳

Life at home was not what I thought it was during that time. I had no idea that Stacy was even more out of control than I knew back then. Years later, he admitted more things to me about those months...

✳ ✳ ✳

Mom, late one night in December, Donny and I made the bar scene together and excluded Tom. I knew I was stretching myself too far and in too many places, especially with you.

Two weeks after Donny moved out from under the pool table, we were still carefully sneaking him in or out without running into you. The bar scene became our A.M.O. (Avoid Mom Operation) to keep him invisible from you.

I knew you could see that I was going down quickly, as my room's disarray reflected my sliding self-esteem. Plus, I couldn't wake up in time to attend school after a night of drinking.

Soon, Christmas vacation arrived, so I called Tom, and his alter-ego, Jaquita, answered. "What's up, bitch?"

"Say, Jaquita, what's happening next week?"

"You cad! Been missin' me, honey?"

"You know it, bitch!"

"To tell you the truth, *this be the week that I be growing older and wiser.*"

"How old will you and Jaquita be, Tom?"

"We be old enough to know better and young enough to do it in style, honey."

By the next night, I had invited Brian, Betty Bedford, K.C., Greta, Ron, Raylene and Paul, the Drama Club president and, of course, Donny. I lured Tom over to my room that night on the pretense of filming Jaquita in a strip routine for a gay movie, and it worked. Tom walked in around 8:30 p.m. dressed as Jaquita, complete with make-up, a black frizzy wig, a red fringed flapper dress, long red gloves and red high heels to match. She pranced around me twirling her long white beads, when everyone suddenly jumped up from hiding and squealed, "Surprise!"

By the party's end, everyone except Tom was happily drunk and gone. Around three a.m., Tom and I were quietly chatting, while sitting on two opposite couches in my garage room. Mom, that's when you popped your head into my garage room.

"Hi. Is everything okay?"

"Just great, Mom!" *You didn't have a clue what was up.*

"That's nice. I'll be up for a while decorating for Christmas."

"Yes, Ma'am."

"Goodnight, boys."

I turned to Tom. "You know, Mom has her heart set on a white, snow flocked Christmas tree, but she can't afford it. She's short of money, because of helping me live here."

"Stacy, *you be* following me, honey. We gonna fix it!" He drove me three blocks, parked near a Christmas tree lot and unlocked his trunk. We wandered past the lot. "No one's here, and *there sits* just the tree your Mom will love."

I stumbled toward the huge tree. "Yeah, that's the one she'd pick out." We looked at each other, grabbed the tree and ran to Tom's car. He opened his unlocked trunk. We stuffed the huge tree inside and sped away.

Tom parked in front of our house. We carried the tree around the side of the house and laid it on the back driveway. I got a hammer, so we could make a tree stand. We hammered on some old wood and tried to make a stand for your new tree. By then, it was four a.m. *"Mom, that's when you opened the pool gate and surprised us."*

"What's all this noise about?"

"We're making a stand for your new Christmas tree."

"Where did you get it, Stacy?"

"We found it!"

"No one *finds* a Christmas tree at four in the morning."

"It must have fallen off a truck or something. It's just what you wanted; a live, white, snow flocked Christmas tree."

"Take it back, Stacy!" *I'm sure my face fell.*

You grinned for a moment. "On second thought, I'm afraid to let you return it. Knowing your luck, you two will get caught and arrested. I'd hate to see both of you spend Christmas in jail, because I can't afford to bail you out. I don't like having a red-hot, stolen Christmas tree, but it sure is pretty."

✳ ✳ ✳

On February 7, 1988, Steve phoned me while I was at work. "Debbie, Crystal went into labor. We are at Freeman Hospital."

I hung up the cafeteria phone and went to find Ivan. "I'm about to be a grandmother again. My daughter went into labor, and I'd like to be there when the baby arrives."

"Can't you wait until you get off work?"

"I must be there when the baby comes. I fought extremely hard to keep this baby alive."

Ivan gave me a funny look. I wasn't in the mood to explain to him what I meant. He heaved a sigh, "Okay, but don't stay gone long." *Gee, this man absolutely has no heart!* I grabbed my gray coat with a faux fur collar, my purse and hurried out to my car.

When I arrived at Freeman Hospital, I was directed to the Nursery Room by a female nurse. Steve was standing there with a huge smile on his face. He gave me a warm hug and pointed out the new arrival. "Take a look at our new little baby boy."

I gazed at our adorable little baby through the window and grinned from ear-to-ear. "He is a sight to behold. What did you two name him?"

"Crystal picked out his name. He is officially Adam Gentry Simmons."

I looked at Steve. "Do you think he could be yours?"

"Nope, but he is now!"

"That's all I wanted to hear." Steve led me to Crystal's hospital room.

I hugged her neck. "You have one beautiful little boy in that Nursery Room, honey."

She nodded. "I know."

I left her room, found the hospital florist, bought some beautiful yellow flowers and returned to Crystal's room. "These flowers are because I love you and my new little grandson so much!"

"Thanks."

"Honey, I have to get back to work. Ivan didn't want to allow me to leave work today, but I insisted. See you later." I scurried outside to my car.

✶ ✶ ✶

It wasn't long before Stacy phoned me early one morning. "Mom, I have someone who wants to say 'Hi' to you."

A bold female voice came through the phone line. "Hi, Mom Malone, I'm Janet Martin."

"Janet, it's nice to meet you via the phone."

Stacy took the phone. "Mom, we have something to tell you."

"Okay."

They jointly yelled through the phone line, "We're getting married!"

Surely this is some kind of prank by Stacy? Why would he want to get married, now that he's Come Out as gay?

"What?" I almost choked. "Stacy, I thought you were gay?"

"I am, but we're in love, Mom."

Janet got on the phone again. "My dad is gay, so I understand Stacy completely. He's in good hands. His *gayness* doesn't bother me. He's such a hunk!"

Nervous laughter was my only response.

"Mom Malone, I'm a hairdresser. Stacy and I met at Red Rock River Park two weeks ago."

"I've become quite familiar with that park recently. So, are you going to elope?"

"Oh, no. I want a big church wedding. I want the works. My brother is an Assistant Pastor at the church right across the street from your house. He's going to marry us there for free."

"I hope you'll take the time to get to know each other first."

"We'll be ready for the ceremony in two weeks. I'm going to borrow my cousin's wedding dress."

"Two weeks? That's rather sudden."

She gushed, "It was true love at first sight."

"Janet, let me talk to Stacy."

She handed him the phone. "Hi, Mom."

"Sweetheart, I wish you'd give this decision more thought."

"Mom, I'm going to bring her there right now, so you can meet her." Then, Stacy hung up. I had no way of knowing, at the time, that Stacy was still high on drugs and booze.

My head was reeling! *Dear God, where will this end?*

Twenty minutes later, Stacy opened our front door and brought Janet into the den. I stood up to shake her hand. She grinned from ear-to-ear, pushed my hand aside and screeched in a loud voice. "Mom!" She grabbed me a big bear hug. "Why don't you come by my salon sometime? I'll cut your hair for free." *I don't know whether to laugh or cry. This is like a bad dream.* I rubbed my forehead in sheer disbelief over the rapid events.

Janet was a short, heavy-set girl with blonde hair who dressed like Madonna. Her huge boobs were mooning back at me. I was dumb-struck. She was all giggles and laughs. "Mom Malone, I want Stacy to stay away from those gay bars and visit my charismatic church."

Stacy grinned, "Why? Is it the lesser of two evils?"

"Honey, I'm counting on you to impress my family, not *depress them.*" Janet took Stacy's hand. "Bye, Mom. We must be off to intro Stacy to my family." They were gone in a flash.

✳ ✳ ✳

I waited a week before I broke the news to my family. *Maybe this wedding idea will fade away as fast as it appeared.*

Sadly, it didn't. I finally phoned Mother and then Crystal. I received the same reaction. Stunned silence, followed by, "I thought he was gay?"

At work that afternoon, I approached my friend, Lori Holland. "Hey, want to go out for lunch tonight? I have some news to tell you."

She gave me a look. "Oh, oh, I can tell by the sound of your voice it isn't good news."

I grinned, "It depends."

After she walked away, I closed my eyes. *It's a good thing none of my friends know that Stacy's gay.*

At supper, I tried to smile at Lori as we ate. "Stacy announced yesterday that he's getting married in two weeks."

She gasped. "Two weeks? How long has he known her?"

"Two days by the sound of things."

Lori threw herself back in her seat. "Oh Lordy!"

"Since I know how to make beautiful cakes, I'll make the bride and groom cakes. I can also make all of the wedding food."

"How can I help you, Debbie?"

"Will you help me decorate the auditorium the night before?"

"Of course, and I'll even loan the happy couple my convertible for their honeymoon."

"That will help a whole lot. I just don't have much spare cash right now, so I have to do as much as I can myself."

"What about a photographer?"

"I don't know. I'll be too busy to take pictures."

"Why not get Sassy Hall to do it? She has a new camera that can also record a video."

"She's just never been very nice to me."

"Let me ask her."

"That's a deal."

I was amazed the next day, when Lori stopped me in the restroom. "Sassy said she'd love to do the pictures and video."

When I got home from work that night, Stacy wasn't there. I watched TV until he arrived at home. "Mom, you're up late."

"I wanted to know if you've broken the news to Tim yet."

"No. I guess it's time to do it."

"Yes, and I don't have the funds to cover your honeymoon."

"I can get Dad to cover that cost." He plopped on the couch. *I could smell alcohol on him. I had no idea, at that time, that he was also doing drugs.*

"Honey, you know I'm floored by this sudden decision. Gays don't marry girls. I guess if you want to try it, I'm willing to help you. Who am I to say that you can't love a girl? After all, you loved Patty so much. I hope it works out."

✷ ✷ ✷

Come morning, I listened as Stacy phoned Tim. "Dad, I have some big news. I'm getting married in a few weeks." *I could almost hear the shock, cynicism and bias in Tim's voice.*

"Well, I'll be there, but are you sure about this? What good will it do, since you're gay? Okay. I'll rent your tuxedo and pay for your wedding night, if you're absolutely sure."

"Dad, we're really in love, so I'm sure."

Stacy began to spend a lot of time at Janet's house across town with her family to discuss their wedding plans. Every day, he gave me an update after I woke up and was dressed.

"Yesterday, I met Janet's Mother. She is a heavyset blonde with a curt personality. Janet's brother, Kevin, is retarded. Tomorrow we begin pre-marital counseling with her older brother, Paul. He's the Assistant Preacher at the Bible Church right across the street. He specializes in marrying and counseling people."

On the second morning, Stacy gave me an update. "Today is our pre-marital counseling with Paul."

"I'll be anxious to hear how it goes, honey."

The following day, Stacy found me at the kitchen table reading the newspaper and sat down in a chair. "Well, Mom, guess what happened to me earlier today."

✳ ✳ ✳

Paul met with Janet first. Afterward, he followed her out the door and put his hand on my left shoulder.

"Stacy, let's walk around outside and have a talk."

While we walked, he pointed at some birds and grass. Then, he gave me his birds-and-bees speech.

"Stacy, God created our birds and grass. God created man to love a woman. God did not create man to love another man. Homosexuality is a sin."

At once, I knew Janet had let my cat out of the bag to her brother.

"You're right, Paul. I am a homosexual, but it isn't a sin. Don't you believe that God created all men?"

"Certainly!"

"Then, God also created homosexuals."

4

≈

Churches and Spirituality

"The Devil turns men into homosexuals through lust and desire," Paul insisted.

"I wish it were that simple."

"It would be a tragic mistake for you to marry Janet, especially since the Devil has you in his grasp."

We ran into Janet, as we re-entered the church building. Her brother took control. "Janet, let's all talk in my office."

We followed him into his office and sat on a couch.

Paul spewed intimidation, as he paced the floor. "Either refrain from this marriage, or God will intervene."

Fire instantly lit Janet's words and her blue eyes. "Oh, *palease!* We're getting married whether *you* like it or not. All I wanted was your blessing."

"I just don't want you to make the same mistake Mom did."

"How could you?"

She ran out of Paul's office. I jumped up and followed her down the hallway. "Screw my brother! We'll do what we want!"

✻ ✻ ✻

Soon, their big wedding was only two days away. I called Mother to ask if they were going to attend. "Hi, Momma, just checking if you and Harry will be at Stacy's wedding."

"I will be there with Harry's sister, Rona. Harry isn't going to attend."

"I understand."

When I hung up, I phoned Crystal. "Will you and your family be attending Stacy's wedding?"

"I guess, but I think it's a bad idea."

Next, I phoned Tim. "Hi, I was wondering if all of your family will be at Stacy's wedding."

"I suppose we'll all be there. What do you think about this wedding?"

"I don't have a clue why Stacy wants to do this."

"Can't you talk him out of it?"

"I can give it one last try, I guess."

I hung up and dialed Janet's number. She answered quickly.

"Janet, please reconsider marrying Stacy. His alcoholism is totally out of control. He's too messed up to get married. And marriage won't change the fact that he's gay."

"Mom Malone, I know what I'm getting. I can change him from being gay." *She has no idea what she's walking into. She's clearly blinded by her Love Addiction.*

"His alcoholism is a serious problem right now, Janet, and both of you are so young. Please reconsider."

"I'll talk to Stacy. I just don't know."

Shortly, Janet arrived at our house. "Stacy, Let's go to Victory Park to talk."

When Stacy returned, I was curious. "What's the verdict?"

We walked around the duck pond and stopped to talk.

"Baby, your mom wants me to back out of the wedding."

"What do you want?"

"I'm scared!"

"I am, too. So let's be scared together and go for it."

"Instantly, a beam of light seemed to shine on her face. Her ear-to-ear grin said it all."

"True love it is, Stacy! We'll show everyone. Our wedding is on!" She giggled.

✳ ✳ ✳

After Janet dropped Stacy off at home, he found me washing clothes. "My friends are giving me a Bachelor Party in an hour."

"Okay, but remember your wedding rehearsal is tomorrow night."

"I'll be there, Mom." Stacy left in a flash.

I drove to the grocery store to buy everything I needed to make the bride and groom cakes and all of the finger foods. I stayed up until the wee hours preparing all of the various colors of cake icing. Stacy still wasn't home when I finally went to bed at two a.m.

The next morning, Tim phoned and woke me up. *"Stacy got arrested again last night. I had to bail him out again."*

"What did he do this time?"

"About three a.m., he dropped Janet off and did a California Roll through a Stop Sign. He was too drunk to write his name on the ticket. He and Officer Sloan had words. Stacy called him a *stupid fucker* and got booked for a DWI. It was six a.m. when I finally brought him home. I can't afford to keep bailing him out of jail."

"Then quit doing it. He has to learn to take responsibility for his behavior, or he will never straighten up." *One of these days, Stacy has to hit a bottom, and I know it won't be pretty.*

✳ ✳ ✳

The final dress rehearsal went without a hitch. After Stacy and I walked home, I started preparing the food and cakes for his wedding.

"Mom, I'm going to go to bed early tonight. I'm tired."

"Sleep late in the morning. Your wedding starts at six p.m. tomorrow afternoon." He nodded and went to his garage room.

I phoned Lori. "Hi, I'll meet you at the church at eight a.m. tomorrow. We can decorate the church lobby and seats then."

"Debbie, I know how excited you must be! Your youngest is about to be a married man."

"It's certainly been exciting so far, that's for sure." I hung up and the phone rang.

"Hi, Debbie, can I speak to Stacy? It's Amy."

"Sure, hold on. I'll tell him to pick up his phone."

I opened Stacy's door. "Stacy, Amy's on the phone for you."

✳ ✳ ✳

It was many years later, when Stacy filled me in on what actually happened to him that night and on his wedding day. "Remember when Amy called me that night? And you picked up the phone and told me I had a call?"

✳ ✳ ✳

When I answered, Amy's *Drill Sergeant Voice* snarled at me. "Malone! I heard you're getting married tomorrow. You can't get married. You're gay!"

"And you're drunk, Amy!"

"Come over to my place, Malone. Some of your friends want to throw you a bachelor party."

It sounded like another opportunity for me to get drunk.

"Amy, I lost my wheels. Come pick me up."

"I don't know if you're worth it, Malone. Be there in a jiff!"

I quietly eased out the side garage door. I could see you through the kitchen windows baking cakes. Amy drove me to her apartment about nine p.m. A small group of my friends were there; Kasey, Jeff, Tom, Don, Amy and I. We spent most of the night getting crazy drunk and doing crystal. Then, the fun began.

"Malone, do you realize how much Janet looks like Patty?"

"Yeah, yeah, a whole lot, except for her blonde hair. Why?"

"You can't bring Patty back by marrying this girl who looks like her. And besides, Malone, you're a fag!"

"Oh, get away from me!"

I brushed her off with my arm. By ten a.m. the next morning, I was still at Amy's house, drunk and high. It was my wedding day, and no one knew where I was. I knew you had stayed up most of the night baking cakes and making decorations. That morning, you and Lori were decorating the church. By eleven a.m., you called all of my friends looking for me.

Promptly at eleven-thirty, Amy drove me to pick up my rented tuxedo and drove me home. My big garage room felt too confining, probably from my crystal high, so I put on my tuxedo and headed into the backyard. That's when you spotted me and came outside.

"What are you doing, Stacy? Your wedding starts in a few hours."

"I'm going to do something for you that Bart never would."

"What, pray tell, would that be?"

"Finish your water fountain. The one he left half-done seven years ago."

"Stacy, you'll get cement all over your tuxedo!"

"Don't worry, Mom. It's the least I can do to repay you for all the work you've done for our wedding."

By five p.m., I had your water fountain almost finished. You stepped out our back door.

"Stacy, it's time to clean up and get yourself to the church."

I agreed and arrived at the church just as Amy did.

"Here, Malone, take this." She handed me more crystal. "You need something to keep you awake for your wedding. It's fifteen minutes till *blast off!*"

"Why am I getting married, Amy?"

"It beats the hell out of me, Malone. Just another crazy thing you're doing."

Shortly after I used the crystal, Janet's mom grabbed my arm and hurried me to the back of the church auditorium. Janet's best friend, Kurt, was the Best Man. Then, the loud organ began to play. Kurt stuck a pink carnation into my lapel. In an instant, rippling PCP flashbacks suddenly rattled my brain. It felt like the *Gates of Hell* were closing in on me from all sides.

✳ ✳ ✳

On March 5, 1988, Stacy and Janet were married. I barely managed to get three hours of sleep the night before their wedding. I dressed and walked across the street to the church. Lori met me at the front door. "Hurry, the wedding party is waiting on you to begin the ceremony."

An escort seated me across the aisle from Tim, his mother, Dana, and his sister, Mona. Mother and Harry's sister, Rona, were seated beside me. Crystal, Steve and little Daniel sat behind us. Then, "The Wedding March" began to play. Stacy finally shared his PCP wedding flashbacks with me…

✳ ✳ ✳

I saw flashbacks throughout the whole wedding event. It was a good thing one of your friends videotaped the wedding. Otherwise, I'd never believe it went so well. From my PCP viewpoint, there were melting candelabras, awkward young ring bearers, goofy relatives, a howling minister, and a chubby bride. I was a nervous gay groom with wide, rolling eyes that stared at nearby wilting flowers for entertainment.

Later, I watched the videotape and realized just how drastically skewed drugs and alcohol had made me that day. The wedding actually looked quite impressive, so I was relieved.

And, your pesky photographer captured our various family groups. The family expressions on all sides of each family were quite telling. They reeked of extreme disapproval.

I was still high during our wedding reception. It appeared to me that we had stuffed cake down each other. Then, I yanked several garters off Janet's leg with my teeth, spilled champagne all over her wedding dress, and watched her wedding bouquet fly into a hundred airplane blossoms, as it floated at a snail's pace through the air, compliments of my PCP flashback.

Again, the video camera captured a different wedding reception version. Frankly, I liked my PCP version better. I thought the reception would never end. Finally, we rushed through the crowd toward Lori's white Le Baron Convertible parked on the side of the church.

Dad's painful expression caught my eye, as we hurried past him. The look on his face spoke volumes. *Son, this wedding isn't going to change anything!*

We were covered with flying birdseed, by the time I opened the car door. Janet's long gown filled up most of the front seat. I slammed her door and hurried to open the driver door. The entire time, I felt like I was trapped in a film noire.

When I stepped on the gas pedal, the car kicked into slow motion and so did the scene in my head. We inched away from the church, birdseed hung in the air; tin cans slowly clanged behind the car; streamers tied to the hubcaps played weird music; multiple voices slowly echoed good wishes; and a *Just Married* sign floated up and landed on the trunk with a long, drawn out ker-thud.

As I turned the car into the street, a police car passed in front of us. Momentarily, I was jolted back to reality. It quickly passed.

I thought, *Oh, God! What if he stops me?* I panicked. *I'm driving while I'm full of champagne and high on crystal. It won't look good on my DWI record.*

Relief swept through me, when the cop simply waved at *The Newlyweds.* After my recent DWI, I wasn't allowed to leave Red Rock County.

You and Lori followed us to our hotel in your car and came inside to take a few pictures. One was of me carrying Janet over the threshold. Another one caught us kissing. The parting shot showed Janet lovingly removing my coat and tie.

Moments after you two left, I peeled out of my tux and popped more champagne open. Within twenty minutes, I had polished off the whole bottle and passed out on our elegant bedspread.

The next morning when I woke up, Janet was curled up in a nearby chair crying and wailing. "Oh, Stacy, we didn't consummate our marriage last night. Our wedding isn't real!"

"Tonight will be soon enough, Janet." *All the while, I knew my eyes must be a mile wide with relief. Oh, thank God I passed out!*

✳ ✳ ✳

"Honey, it's probably a good thing that I didn't know all of that, or I would have stopped your wedding for sure."

✳ ✳ ✳

Four days passed. Crystal dropped by the house. "Mom, I want to give you something." She handed me a brochure. "We've joined this church, and we'd like for you to come visit this Sunday."

I studied the brochure. It was for a church I'd never heard of before; The Church on the Rock. I smiled. "Okay, I'd like to go this Sunday. How did you hear about this church?"

"Our new babysitter, Karen, invited us. She loves this church and told us all about it and their preacher."

Crystal left as swiftly as she had arrived.

✳ ✳ ✳

On their third morning of marriage, Stacy phoned me. "Mom, we just rented an apartment only five blocks from you."

"How can you afford an apartment so soon?"

"Dad paid our apartment deposit and first month's rent. We have a one-bedroom apartment on the second floor.

Janet's best friend, Curt, and I carried her prize possession upstairs, it was her antique barber chair. Right now, we're putting away wedding gifts and dealing with the newness of marriage."

"That all sounds fine. Now, all you need is a good job."

"I'm going to apply at a new restaurant downtown tomorrow. Janet just moved her license to another hair salon closer to our apartment."

"Let me know when you want to get your things. I have a friend with a truck who can help you get moved."

"I'll call you tomorrow and let you know."

✳ ✳ ✳

Stacy didn't call the next day. The following day was Sunday. I dressed for church and drove to The Church on the Rock. I walked inside, found Crystal, Steve and Daniel and sat beside Crystal. "Where are Wayne and Adam?"

"They're in the church nursery room. I want to introduce you to Karen later. She works in there."

I nodded, as the service began. Preacher Jackson walked onstage and led a rousing, lengthy prayer. Many people in the service began to stand up and chant words that sounded like a weird language. I turned to Crystal and discovered she was also standing up, waving her hand and speaking strange words. *This is not what I expected to see. I can't believe my daughter is participating in this stuff.*

After the service ended, we walked to the nursery door. Crystal went inside to get Wayne and Adam. She returned carrying Wayne, and a tall, homely girl followed her holding little Adam.

Crystal turned to me. "Mom, this is Karen Martin, our new babysitter."

She shook my hand. "I have heard *a lot* about you, Ms. Austin."

"All good, I hope."

She didn't reply and gave me an annoyingly smug expression and a roll of her eyes. We walked outside the building, and I turned to Crystal. "She looks too young to be babysitting three little kids."

"Oh Mother, she has two children and a husband. She's great with our kids!"

✳ ✳ ✳

On Monday, I opened the front door and picked up a letter from my mailbox. The handwriting looked familiar, but the return address certainly didn't. It came from Bowman Prison. I walked inside, sat on the couch and opened Bart's letter.

"Hi, goodlookin', I bet you weren't expecting to hear from me here in Club Fed. I had a little problem, and here I am getting free room-and-board courtesy of you taxpayers again. Ha!

A new friend of mine, named David Golden, asked me if he could leave a bunch of his guns in my Blazer Chalet for a week. I didn't see the harm and agreed. Three nights later, the Feds raided my truck and arrested me. I told them that the guns belonged to a friend. They just didn't believe me, so here I am once again, because I helped out a buddy."

"Shucks, you know me. I'm just a good ol' boy. Right? Anyway, I will likely be here for a few years, unless I can get out on good behavior. Hah! I sure do love you! Always, Bart."

Good behavior? I doubt Bart knows the meaning of good behavior. I refolded the letter, slipped it back inside the envelope and shook my head. *Will Bart ever learn to stay out of trouble? Why can't I stop my feelings for this sick man?*

The following day, Stacy phoned. "Mom, I'm ready to move my things today. Is your friend with a truck available?"

"I'll check with him and let you know." I phoned my favorite dancing friend named Dick. He showed up thirty minutes later, so I phoned Stacy. "Honey, Dick's here with his truck. Get over here and help him load your things."

In less than four hours, Stacy's furniture, clothing, and other items were gone from his garage room. As they were about to leave with the last load, he turned and handed me a large unicorn statue. "Is this for me?"

"I know how much you love them, and I wanted you to have it. Do you like it?"

"Like it? I love it! Thank you, sweetheart!" I hugged Stacy's neck.

"I'll call you to come see our apartment, after we get it arranged."

"Great, I can't wait."

Stacy phoned me two days later, "Mom, Janet is at work. I want you to come see our apartment."

It only took me five minutes to arrive at Stacy's door. I knocked, and he let me inside. "Here it is, Mom. It's all finished." He gave me a tour of their apartment. The standout area was a smallish room with many windows where Stacy had placed Janet's antique barber chair.

Unexpectedly, Stacy sighed. "Mom, Janet's living in total fantasy. She thinks I am the most wonderful thing ever. And I keep asking myself, *how can I get out of this mess without hurting her?* All doubt about me being gay has now been totally erased. I have no ability to love Janet. Her similarities to Patty were what had attracted me to her."

Relief swept through me like a cool, summer breeze. I hope this marriage will be over in a month or two.

"I always thought you were in love with Patty."

"In retrospect, I wasn't sure I was gay when I was with Patty. When Janet showed up, and we got married, it cleared up any lingering doubts. Now, *I know I am gay.*"

"So what are you going to do, honey?"

"Dad just promised to buy me another new car, so I don't know what to do. Tomorrow will be our first Friday morning together, and it's also my DWI Court date."

"Honey, it's also Friday the Thirteenth."

"Oh boy, a triple whammy!"

✻ ✻ ✻

When I returned home, my phone was ringing. "Debbie, I need a big favor. This Saturday is my hubby Frank's birthday. I want to surprise him. Will you come over and do your belly dance for him?"

"Sure, if I can bring Jay. He's been dying to see me dance."

I hung up. The phone rang again. This time it was Mother. "Hi, we're on the way there to take you and Crystal's family to lunch. They are on their way to your house."

They arrived promptly at noon. Crystal showed up ten minutes later with Daniel, Wayne and little Adam. We decided to take two cars and went to a famous cafeteria. On the way back, Harry rode with Crystal and Adam. Daniel, Wayne and I rode with Mother. Unexpectedly, Daniel leaned forward from the backseat and tapped my arm. "Nana, Mom told us that we can't come to your house anymore."

I whipped around toward him. *"She said what?"*

"We can't come to your house anymore."

"Why not?"

"Because you have *Demonic Unicorns!" My mind wanted to explode! Where in the hell did Crystal get this ludicrous crap?*

5

≈

Either Laugh or Cry

The moment Mother parked her car, I stepped out and waited for Crystal to park her SUV. She opened her passenger door. Adam was in his car seat. She helped Daniel and Wayne inside and turned to hug Harry. I approached her. "What's this nonsense about me having *Demonic Unicorns*, and I can't see my grandchildren anymore?"

She snapped, "It isn't nonsense. Preacher Jackson told us about it. Unicorns are evil!" *I should have known. This irrational garbage came from that cult church preacher.*

"That's ludicrous nonsense and you know it."

Demonic Unicorns???

"I don't have to listen to you!" Crystal wheeled around, hopped into her SUV and drove away.

I was so angry, I could have spit nails! *What kind of preacher tries to split families because of unicorns?*

After Mother and Harry left, I went inside and phoned Jay. I told him about Crystal's insane accusation about me having *evil unicorns,* and that she has banned me from seeing her family again. I didn't think he was ever going to quit laughing. "Stop it, Jay! This isn't funny. Her church is trying to split up my family by brainwashing my daughter."

"You're right, baby. I'm sorry. Let me take you to lunch, so you can calm down."

Jay showed up at my front door thirty minutes later. When I opened the door, he rushed inside. "Wait until you see what I found on the Internet." He hurried into my kitchen and spread out three pages across the table. "Look at this article. *Cult Churches Use all of these as Demonic; Frogs, Crystals, Triangles, Owls, Candles, Horseshoes and Shamrocks! It is Mind Control.*"

Next, he placed five more pages on the table. *Unicorns Symbolize Purity, Grace, Innocence, Healing and Truth.* "They also symbolize Christ who was a *Miracle and a Mystery of Nature.* The King James Bible mentions unicorns in seven different places. So much for Crystal's Preacher Jackson and his Demonic Unicorns."

Instantly, I threw my arms around Jay's neck and kissed him. "This is why I'm so crazy about you! You always help me find a bright spot in every bad moment with my family. Thank you!"

He gave me his best sexy grin, "Does this mean I get to give my special baby a *kiss massage* tonight?"

I blushed, "Oh, yeah!"

✳ ✳ ✳

When I woke up at Jay's, I realized it was Friday. I hit the floor running. I had to drive Stacy and Janet downtown to the County Court building for his DWI hearing. I parked in an underground lot. We rode the elevator to the third floor. Stacy left us in the hallway on a church pew, while he went to visit an Assistant D.A.

Fifteen minutes later, he returned and told us what had just happened. "An attractive Brooke Shields-looking, Assistant D.A. named Christine invited me to sit at her desk."

"If you insist on representing yourself today, I suggest you consider accepting my offer."

"What does that involve?"

"It's Deferred Adjudication with a two-year probation, and my driver's license is suspended for nine months. You will be assigned a Probation Officer, and you *must* report every month. Until agreed, you cannot leave Red Rock County. Also, you must stay employed and get counseling for your drinking problem."

My wheels began to spin. Do I agree or go it on my own?

"Well, young man?"

"I suppose so."

"Then, she gave me a tip."

"Prepare yourself. Judge Dixon will try to scare you to see your reaction, so be ready!"

"I signed a document to accept her offer. Now, it's time for me to go see Judge Dixon." Stacy led us into a small DWI Courtroom. We sat on the second row.

A surly Court Bailiff announced, "Malone!"

I watched Stacy rise with a wistful look and walk through a half-gate. He stopped in front of Judge Dixon. He was a semi-balding man with a distinct Jack Nicholson-type scowl. "Are you representing yourself today, Mr. Malone?"

"Yes, I am, Sir."

"How do you plead?"

"I plea bargained with the Assistant D.A. and accepted Deferred Adjudication, a two-year probation and other terms on her offer, Sir."

There was a long, heart-stopping pause, while Judge Dixon read the document handed to him by the Court Bailiff. Then, he stared over his half-moon glasses and scowled at Stacy. "You know, son, *I could put you in prison for two years.*"

I could barely hear Stacy's quivering voice reply, "Yes, Sir."

"Can you tell me why I shouldn't?"

"Yes, Sir, I'm a newlywed. My bride and my mother are here today." He pointed at us over his left shoulder. "I'm back in high school, and I just started a new job. I'm trying so hard, Your Honor."

I watched Judge Dixon try to put the *Fear of God* in Stacy. He stared at him and tapped his fingers on his desk for the longest time. Stacy seemed to be looking at a U.S. flag beside Judge Dixon. I held my breath. Finally, I heard his wooden gavel strike his desk like a cannon. "Granted! Bailiff, next case."

A long sigh escaped my lips. Janet and I turned and followed Stacy into the hallway. He beamed, "I guess I passed the test!"

I didn't raise my kids to lie. I totally detest dishonesty. "You flunked the test about no lying. You aren't in school."

"I know, Mom."

"What if he finds out you lied to him?"

"What can he do?"

"Put you in prison!"

"Oh, Mom, let's go home."

Janet hung on his arm like a lovesick puppy with moon-shaped eyes. "Oh, Stacy, you were so wonderful in there!"

✳ ✳ ✳

After Stacy's day in Judge Dixon's Court, I was ready for some fun. I pulled out my belly dance costume, long blond wig, zeals and tape recorder that was loaded with my Greek music. It took me about an hour to dress and do my make-up. Jay rang my doorbell promptly at seven p.m. He saw me and whistled. "Hub-bah, hub-bah!" Then, he escorted me to his car, drove me to Lori's house and parked.

"Sweetie, go ring their doorbell and tell Lori that I'm ready to surprise Frank." He left me in the car and did as I asked.

Lori stepped outside her front door, waved and pointed to her open garage door. Then, she took Jay inside. I slipped in their garage and pantry door. I heard her say to Frank, "Honey, close your eyes. I saved your best birthday surprise for last." Soon, she turned on my dance music. I came dancing into their living room playing my zeals and fully wrapped in my veil. Jay was draped across a large cushioned footrest. He was drooling so much over my dance that I got tickled for a moment. Lori prompted Frank. "Open your eyes!"

As I whirled and weaved my veil toward Frank, I made a colorful canopy over his head and swiveled for him. He actually blushed. My routine only lasted five minutes, but everyone loved it. It was a wonderful evening of stress relief for me.

✳ ✳ ✳

The next day, I called The Church on the Rock. "I want an appointment to see Preacher Jackson." I was given 2:30 p.m.

When I arrived, the Church Secretary escorted me to his office. We shook hands, and I sat down. "How can I help you, Ms. Austin?"

"You told my daughter not to come see me again, until I got rid of my *Demonic Unicorns*. Churches do not split families."

"You are mistaken. The Bible says in *Luke 12:51-53; Do you think that I have come to give Peace on Earth? No, I tell you, but rather division.*"

"That verse does not mention unicorns. Here are some Bible verses you *are ignoring.* The King James Bible mentions unicorns *nine times. Numbers 23:22; 24:8; Deuteronomy 33:17; Job 39:9-10; Psalms 22:21; 29:6; 92:10; Isaiah 34:7.* The only thing that's demonic here is *you* for trying to brainwash my daughter and split up my family. I will not tolerate what you are trying to do to my family."

"You can't stop me!"

"Don't be so sure!" I stood up and left his office. *What I really wanted to do was box his ears to knock some sense into his empty head for sounding like a lunatic instead of a real preacher.*

✳ ✳ ✳

Stacy phoned me during his third week of marriage. "Mom, can my landlady kick us out of our apartment for having a party?"

"It depends on what was going on at your party."

"We threw a Punk Rock party for our friends. Janet dyed my hair blue-black and spiked it. I wore three earrings on each ear, white make-up, dark eyeliner and black lips, donned my white ruffled shirt, black bow tie and long black Dracula cape. I was a Punk Rock Vampire."

"Okay, but were you too noisy or drinking or what?"

"No, I was just playing *Rocky Horror* music, and we drank some punch and stuff."

"Then, what did she complain about?"

"I jumped off of our balcony wearing my cape and landed on her prized lilies. I don't remember what I was singing." *My instinct tells me there is a lot more to Stacy's story than he wants to admit to me, so far.*

"Honey, you could have broken both legs. Was that her only complaint?"

"No, she claimed that our neighbors were threatening to move if she didn't stop our party. She told me we'd have to move if it happened again."

"You can't afford to rent another apartment and come up with a deposit."

"I know. We'll be careful."

"That's the smart thing to do. I can't give you money I don't have."

✳ ✳ ✳

My next week was full of fun dates with Jay. We drove to my hometown and visited with Mother and Harry. He kept me laughing the whole time and lifted my spirits. On Friday night after we went dancing, he took me to his apartment for the night. Unfortunately, he got so drunk that he became verbally abusive. I couldn't accept another abusive alcoholic in my life, so I made him take me home. "Jay, I can't see you anymore." *I pray that I never have another alcoholic in my life again, as long as I live.*

✳ ✳ ✳

On Friday, April 15, 1988, my bedroom phone rang.

"Mother, I want you to come to *The Church on the Rock.*"

"Why should I go there?"

"I want to talk to you."

"Okay." *I feel certain this is not going to be a friendly visit, but I'm not one to run from any situation that threatens the harmony in my family.*

I grabbed my purse and drove to her church. When I walked inside, I was directed to their big gym/auditorium. Crystal was sitting on a chair holding little Adam. He was only ten-weeks-old. Her babysitter, Karen, was sitting beside her. I could see about ten other people across the gym. I sat in the empty chair waiting for me in front of them and put my purse on the floor. "Okay, I'm here. What's this about?"

Crystal launched into an angry diatribe. "You were a horrible Mother. You never touched me, kissed me or loved me. Karen says that means you were an abusive parent!"

"I did the best I could with what I had been given. It was a whole lot more than I ever received from my mother. She's the one who never touched me, showed me any love or warmth of any kind. Over the years, I've had to force myself to touch people, and it always feels weird to me when I do. I can't help how I was raised, but I love you very much!"

"No, you don't. You were *never there for me!*"

"Never? Oh, that's not true! I was there for you more times than I can count. You're just mad at me, because I refused to go along with your sordid lifestyle choices. And, don't forget, you wanted to abort that little guy sitting in your lap, missy!"

"You're disgusting!"

"What's disgusting is that I'm listening to my child who has suddenly developed major memory loss over her past behavior. Do marital affairs ring a bell, or genital warts? Dusted drugs? The list goes on." I grabbed my purse and stood up. "Since I'm such a *Bad Mother, go find yourself another mother!*" I pivoted and left.

When I got home, I phoned Mother and told her the whole sordid story about my visit with Crystal and her nutty Preacher Jackson. "I'm not about to let some lunatic preacher brainwash my daughter by claiming that unicorns are evil and succeed in stopping me from seeing my grandkids."

Mother paused for a moment. "What would it hurt to get rid of them?" *Mother's stance is so predictable. When has she ever gone to bat for me? Maybe once or twice in my entire lifetime.*

"Not only is that not happening, I may go buy more unicorns."

Mother sighed, "Oh, dear me."

I hung up, went through my home and took down every picture of Crystal I could find and put them in a drawer. *I swear, when it rains in my life, it's more like a monsoon! Guess I need to go buy a super umbrella.*

✳ ✳ ✳

It got to the point where I hated to answer my phone anymore. When it rang five days later, I let it ring six times, before I answered it. "Mom, I need to ask you something. Is there any way I can move back home?"

"I don't know, Stacy. Let's talk about it. I'll come over."

As I parked my car, Stacy opened my passenger door and sat in the seat. He appeared to be lower than low.

"What's happened, honey?"

"I lost my wife, got fired from my job, because I spent five days in detox. I was beat up outside Kroger's for stealing food, and the charges are pending. I had to sell my car. My Apartment Manager wants me to move out in three days. I have nowhere to go."

"I can't let you come home while you're drinking."

"What can I do, Mom?"

"Tell me, Stacy, what else do you have to lose now?"

"Only my life." *Thank you, God. It sounds like Stacy has finally hit his bottom!*

✳ ✳ ✳

After my friend, Dick, helped Stacy move back home, he grinned at me. "When are you going dancing again?"

"Tomorrow night sounds good. I'll see you there at eight."

After Dick left, I looked at Stacy. "Time to sit down on the couch and tell me what happened to end your marriage."

"I'm as surprised as you, or maybe you *aren't surprised,* since I'm gay. Here's what happened..."

✳ ✳ ✳

We had a big party at our apartment one night. I was in my Dracula cape and make-up. Everything seemed normal, after I returned from the liquor store, until I saw Amy. I plopped down in Janet's barber chair, rolled it side-to-side with my foot and gave her a hard stare.

"Janet, how did Amy end up here?"

"Oh, I called her to come join us. No biggie."

She shrugged her chubby shoulders a bit nervously. I stood up and walked to the turntable to play a different record.

Suddenly, a thundering knock hit our door. I pushed it ajar and peered through the slit sideways. I saw three middle-aged men in gray suits staring at my painted face. One had a paper in hand. "Are you Stacy Malone?"

"Yes, I am. What's the matter?"

"We have an Arrest Warrant for you, Mr. Malone."

"I thought I took care of that. I'm on probation."

"What are you talking about?"

"Aren't you here about my DWI?"

He looked perplexed.

"No, you have an appointment with a doctor."

"Doctor? What doctor?"

Hysterical crying erupted directly behind me.

"Why do I need a doctor?"

I glanced over my shoulder to see Janet sobbing and Amy comforting her.

"We have an Arrest Warrant against you for a Mental Health Citation, Mr. Malone."

"What do you mean? I'm not crazy!"

"Your wife doesn't agree. She's afraid you might be suicidal."

Next, I heard more hysterical crying behind me.

"Mr. Malone, she says you believe you're Frank N. Furter from *Rocky Horror Picture Show*. Remove all your jewelry."

I turned toward the coffee table, glared at Janet and removed my jewelry, when a pair of handcuffs gripped my wrists.

"Janet wailed, 'Oh Stacy!' "

The Officers grabbed my shoulders and pushed me toward the doorway. I stopped at the threshold and turned to look back at the weeping group. "Oh, I feel just like Blanche DuBois! I've always depended on the kindness of strangers."

Once in the unmarked police car, the *Redneck Officers* drove me to Freeman Hospital. They proudly wore their sarcasm.

"What kinds of music do you like, Malone?" They put their radio on a country music station.

"Do you like George Jones?"

"Not particularly."

"We didn't think so. What kind of music does a *Dracula Clone* like anyway?"

I ignored them, and their sick jokes. They led me inside the hospital, still handcuffed and walked me toward a big, yellow arrow on the wall pointing to a *Psychiatric Ward.*

✷ ✷ ✷

Several black people were milling around in the long hallway. One of them mouthed off at me. "Okay, brother. That's where *Dracula Guy* needs to go, to the Psych Ward!"

I was led around the corner into a holding cell area. Five nurses ran to the glass to stare at me, my clothes and garish make-up. Then, Head Nurse Maude approached me.

"Empty your pockets. Take off your belt. Do you have any weapons?"

"No, Miss Maude."

"Nurse Maude to you."

She marched me into a small waiting room and locked the door. Another stream of nurses peered at me through the glass. I smiled back at them. *Now I know how monkeys in the zoo feel.*

Nurse Maude returned with a clipboard and questions. "What's your problem?"

"It's my wife. *Apparently, she has a problem.* Not me!"

She escorted me outside the room to sit in the hall. "Here's the drill, Malone. Two doctors, an internist and a staff psychologist will make an evaluation. Depending upon their opinions, you could be admitted to Russell State Mental Hospital for a minimum of ninety days or a maximum of nine months."

I looked at her with sad eyes. "Can I wash my face first? I'm afraid the doctors won't take me seriously, otherwise."

"Okay, but I have to watch you. Can't have you try to kill yourself."

She led me to a restroom and stared at me, as I removed my Dracula make-up, flattened my hair and quickly returned to normal. She actually loaned me her comb.

"Thanks, Nurse Maude. What types of people are in Russell?"

"You'll mostly see suicides, manic depressives, psychopaths and homeless people needing a place to live at County expense for nine months."

Then, she returned me to the hallway. I tried to rehearse answers for the doctors. Suddenly, a heavyset *Senorita* came rushing toward me. "Hi, I'm Esmeralda. I've been looking everywhere for you."

Two male nurses rushed down the hall toward her.

"Sit down, Esmeralda."

"Go to hell, weirdoes! This is my brother, Lupe."

She screamed and dove at me. The male nurses wrestled her to the floor, restrained her, shoved her into a holding room and locked the door. She pounded on the door for thirty minutes. Then, she burst into a Spanish song and stared at me through the window. *I wonder if Lupe knows his sister is crazy.*

After three hours, an Internist led me into an office and took the only chair, so I sat on a comfortable loveseat.

"Do you know why you're here, Stacy?"

"I think my wife is a bit upset, because I'm a homosexual."

A look of unexpected understanding passed between us. Tension cleared the room. "Oh, you're gay!"

An unspoken bond telegraphed that he, too, was gay. Our interview became more like gossip.

"Did your wife know you were gay when she married you?"

"Sure, we met in a nearby gay park, Red Rock River Park."

"Why did you marry her?"

"I don't know. I thought maybe I loved her. She's a nice girl. I thought being married could fix things for me. Patty would have married me, if I'd proposed to her, before she was killed by a hit-and-run driver. You know if..." *Those awful words about Patty's death still rip my heart apart.*

The Internist never mentioned my Dracula attire. Instead, he zeroed in on Janet. "Isn't it a little odd that a nice young girl would intentionally marry a homosexual?"

"I suppose."

Suddenly, a Psychiatrist joined us. He resembled a middle-aged Sam Elliott, with salt-and-pepper hair and a mustache. After they talked, the Internist handed the Psychiatrist his clipboard and disappeared. He closed the door and sat down."

"I'm Dr. Rex Wills. I hear you're a married homosexual, and your wife is upset about that."

"That's right, Dr. Rex."

"Are you aware, Mr. Malone, that your wife wrote on her petition that you are psychotic, and you think you are Frank N. Furter from *Rocky Horror Picture Show?*"

A knowing smile crossed my face. "That's no surprise."

"Clearly, the way you are dressed could lead someone to that conclusion. True?"

"I could see that, Sir."

"Do you think that you *are* Frank N. Furter?"

"Certainly not!"

"Tell me why were you were dressed that way."

"We go to a club called *Sparkles*. It's a teen bar. People there dress that way."

"Then, this is the style for that club?"

"Yes, Sir. I've dressed like this for a long time. Many times, I played Frank N. Furter at the Red Rock Stage Theater, and sometimes, I played other characters. Part of the fun was dressing up for the show. Afterward, we liked to go into public places for the shock value."

"Shock value?"

"Yes, Sir. Can you see why?"

"Yes, yes, I can see why people would be shocked."

"I remember from my high school psychology class that psychos can't tell the difference between right and wrong. I know the difference, Sir."

Dr. Rex peered at his clipboard, made several written notes and continued. "Do you have any suicidal thoughts?"

"None."

"Have you ever been violent or hit your wife?"

"Never."

"Any idea why your wife married you, knowing you're gay?"

I gazed upward in search of divine guidance. "Maybe it was because of her father."

"What about her father?"

"He's gay. Maybe she's searching for a father replacement."

Dr. Rex shook his head and scribbled more notes. "I think I'm more concerned about why your wife would act this way, knowing you were gay. I believe you're stable and no threat to yourself or others. The person who seems to need psychiatric help is Janet, not you. Would you sign papers to commit her?"

"Absolutely not!"

"Why not?"

"I don't believe it's fair to do that to anyone, even though she did it to me."

Dr. Rex momentarily looked flushed, and then, he began to write on his clipboard.

"I'm recommending your discharge. Your wife and a friend named Amy are waiting in the hall to take you home."

"Home? Me? Oh, okay. I'll go with them."

"Stacy, do you mind if I talk to Janet before you leave?"

"Fine with me, Dr. Rex, but I'm not signing papers on her. He wrote out a discharge slip, signed it and handed it to me to sign. I signed, shook his hand at the door and left.

"Unexpectedly, Janet rushed up and grabbed my hand."

"Oh Stacy, I'm sorry. You're not mad at me, are you?"

"No, no, but the doctor wants to talk to you."

"Me?" She sounded excited.

I nodded with a smile and looked at Amy. "I'm going to the restroom. I'll be right back." I hurried down the hallway and turned left out the Emergency Door." *Freedom at last!*

✳ ✳ ✳

It was exactly midnight. I walked twelve blocks to Red Rock River Park. Instantly, Tom spotted me sitting on a real red rock bench near the spot where I had proposed to Janet. "Hey, Stacy, come ride in my van. I've got mucho booze."

Insanity whispered in my ear, "Back to the bottle. Forget Janet!"

I stood up and walked to Tom's van. "Gee, Tom, you're dressed like a nighttime *Mommy Dearest* and doin' the great Joan Crawford tonight."

"Shut up and get in, you insane bitch!"

"Me, insane? I'm sitting in a yellow-and-black van with my friend, Tom. His face is covered with dots of cold cream. A black hairnet is wrapped over his pink sponge hair rollers. His white silk bathrobe is gaping open to reveal an overly hairy chest on his skinny body, and his size ten feet are sporting white silk-and-feather house slippers. So, who's the crazy one here?"

Tom rolled down his van window and yelled out at numerous gays walking in the park, "Don't fuck with me, fellas! I'm on a warpath, *'cause I'm Mommy Dearest, and I'm headin' your way!*"

6

≈

Sometimes It Takes a Stubborn Bitch

Stacy's one month marriage was soon over after a quick divorce. I agreed to drive him to-and-from his Probation Officer every month, because he'd lost his car.

In the meantime, I tired of Crystal's *Demonic Unicorn* scam to keep me away from my grandchildren. Three months later, I picked up my phone and called Steve's father. "Hi Garrett, are you aware of what's been going on with Crystal, Steve and my grandchildren?"

"No, I haven't heard anything. What's happening?"

"They got involved with *The Church on the Rock*. Their preacher convinced them that I had *Demonic Unicorns*, and that I should never be allowed to see any of them again, until I destroyed all of them. It's like brainwashing. Would you talk with Steve and see if you can put a stop to this craziness? No grandparent should have to put up with this kind of nonsense."

"Of course, I will. That's the weirdest thing I've ever heard of in my life."

Garrett must have called Steve immediately. The next night at work, I looked up to see Crystal and Steve approach me in my work area. She was carrying flowers, a card and wearing a friendly smile. "Mom, I'd like for us to be a family again."

Happiness swept through me. I hugged both of them. "This is the best news I've had in a long time." *I was soon participating in their family activities again and loving every minute of it.*

✳ ✳ ✳

Stacy was still without wheels, so I gave him my old green Chevy that Mother and Harry had given to me for when he was able to drive a car again. That way, he could find a job. In days, he was hired at an Italian restaurant on Holland Street.

One day, I was mowing my front yard and my neighbor, John Scherer, waved at me. "Debbie, I want you to know I found Stacy passed out in his Chevy with the door wide open last night. I did my usual, put him inside his car and closed the door before a cop drove by and arrested him. You know I'm in AA. Stacy needs some serious help. His blackouts will only get worse."

I finished mowing, went inside, peeked into Stacy's garage room and gathered his clothes. They reeked of alcohol. I dressed for work and waited until he woke up. He wandered into the den at three p.m. I looked at him. *Shades of Tim, he's hung over.*

"It's time for an AA meeting."

He mumbled. "Not right now, Mother. I just woke up."

"Yeah, and look what time it is. It's past time for you to attend an AA meeting."

He plopped on the couch. "I'm gay. I don't want to go to a *straight* AA meeting."

"Okay, I'll find you a gay AA meeting."

I picked up the Yellow Pages and found a listing for many AA meetings. I dialed their main number, while Stacy ate some cereal and drank a glass of milk. "Hello, I need to find a gay AA group. Can you help me?"

I spoke to an understanding man. "Yes, there is a large group called Lambda. They have meetings three times a day; 10:00 a.m., 8:00 p.m., and 11:00 p.m. They're the group for you."

I chuckled. "No, it's for my son. Thanks." I hung up and turned to Stacy. "We're in luck. They have a big gay group called Lambda."

Stacy finished off his milk. "I'm not going, unless you go with me, Mom."

"No problem. I'll take you there. They have a meeting at 8:00 p.m. tonight."

✱ ✱ ✱

I will never forget watching Stacy dress for his first gay AA meeting. He put on his worn jeans, black boots with chains, punk rock t-shirt and black leather jacket covered with at least two hundred Punk Rock pins. Then, he applied heavy black Gothic makeup, a spiked dog collar and bracelets, many earrings, and spiked his dark hair.

We walked to my car, and I drove him to a local hotel where the Lambda meetings were held near an airport. When we arrived, we were directed upstairs to the main meeting room. I had no idea what to expect. We climbed the stairs to the room, I opened the meeting door and turned to Stacy, "Go find a seat. I'll wait downstairs."

A nice looking man overheard me. "This is an Open Meeting. You can come in with your son tonight." As I entered behind Stacy, I suddenly felt like a magnet. All eyes turned and focused, not on Stacy, but on me. I had no idea why.

Years later, I learned that any parent who attends a gay AA meeting in support of their child is a true rarity. I still find that fact to be a great sadness about this world. I love my son, gay or straight!

✱ ✱ ✱

Two months passed when I received a phone call.

"Hi goodlookin', I'm out of Club Fed, have a job and an apartment. I'd like for you to come down and visit me sometime. I still love you." *You still love me? Sure you do! Me and how many other women do you still love, including my daughter?*

"I don't think that's a good idea, Bart."

"I promise. No strings attached. I'll pay your airfare."

"No, I'll pass. Thanks!"

"If you change your mind, just call me."

"Keep your money. You need it." *The Snake Charmer just can't accept that I'm no longer an easy mark for his charisma.*

✳ ✳ ✳

At work, I heard some upsetting news when I walked in the door. Lori approached me. "Did you know that Adelle is sick?"

"I know she's been complaining about a stomach ache."

"She's having surgery tomorrow."

The next day, we waited anxiously for news about Adelle's surgery. Her daughter, Maggie, called me on our cafeteria phone. "Things didn't go as expected. The doctors opened Mom up and closed her up."

"Why would they do that?"

"They discovered that her ovaries are shot full of cancer."

I gulped. "Oh, no!" I hung up and turned to find Lori waiting to hear what happened. "Apparently, the doctors found that Adelle's cancer is so widespread that they just closed her up."

The news was unbearable. I walked into our work area and found Johnny in his office. My tears began to flow. He stood up and approached me. "What's happened?"

"Adelle helped me through my nightmare with Bart. Now, her doctors say there's no hope. She's dying of ovarian cancer."

Johnny gave me a hug. "I know how close you two have been over the years."

I nodded. "This is so wrong."

He lifted my chin. "I care about you more than as just a friend. If I weren't married, I'd be a whole lot more to you."

"Thank you for caring. It means more than you know."

"Getting that out of me is like getting blood out of a turnip."

I smiled at him through my tears. "How well I know."

✳ ✳ ✳

Things with Crystal and her family were actually stabilized. She and I took the kids to a Mall to meet up with Mother and Harry. As we walked through the mall, Daniel and Wayne found a water fountain and sat on the wide edge. I took their picture.

"Crystal, take one of me with the boys."

She had Adam in a stroller. Mother took it over, so Crystal could take our picture. Suddenly, I saw Mother put her hand to her heart. "I need to sit down and rest for a while."

I helped her to a nearby bench. "Are you tired, or are you having chest pains?"

"No, I think I'm just winded. I'll be fine."

She and Harry decided to cut their visit short. We walked them outside to their car. After they drove away, Crystal frowned. "Has that ever happened to her before?"

"Not that I know of, but Mother doesn't always tell me things. She knows I will take action, if there's a problem."

✳ ✳ ✳

It wasn't long until Stacy came home happy after an AA meeting. "Mom, I finally picked an AA Sponsor. His name is Bradley D."

"That's great news. What made you choose him?"

"He's a *Big Book Thumper who tells it like it is.* I know that's exactly the kind of AA Sponsor I need."

"I'd like to meet him sometime."

"That's good. He wants to meet you right away."

✳ ✳ ✳

Two days later, Stacy found me typing on my computer at the kitchen table. "Mom, tonight is an Open Meeting. Bradley asked me to bring you there to meet him."

"Let me finish typing my pages, and I'll go get ready."

An hour later, we arrived at Lambda and walked upstairs to their Open Meeting. I saw a crowd of mostly gay men and a few females standing in a circle talking. Stacy led me toward the crowd. "Bradley, this is my mom."

A tall, blondish haired man, in a colorful silk shirt wheeled around. His booming voice was melodic. "She's just as I pictured her." He wrapped his arms around me in a warm hug. *I felt as if I had just been hugged by an Angel.* "Stacy and I will be spending lots of time together. We're off to a good start."

"That's music to my ears. I believe AA will save his life."

"It will if he stays with it. It's a Spiritual Program that works miracles. I know. I've been sober over twenty-five years."

When the meeting began, we all three sat together. After an hour, the speaker ended the meeting. "Is there anyone here who wants to receive a Serenity Chip?"

I watched as Stacy walked forward with several other young men and took his first chip.

Bradley whispered, "It's a start, but he has a ways to go."

Next everyone stood up, held hands and repeated *The Serenity Prayer.* Then they added, "Keep coming back. It works!"

While Stacy talked with one of the young men who also went up for his Serenity Chip, Bradley took me aside. "Your son is in the right place. It sometimes takes a while to stay sober."

"Anytime you need my help, please call me." I gave him my card with my telephone number.

✳ ✳ ✳

A quiet month passed. Crystal phoned. "Next week is Daniel and Wayne's birthday. Can you come to their party at Chunky Cheese?"

"Of course, I can. What time?"

"Four p.m. It's the one closest to where you live."

"Any ideas on what they want for their birthday?"

"You know little boys. They love cars or trucks. Daniel adores anything that's Ninja Turtle."

"I'll be there with bells on."

I had as much fun watching Daniel and Wayne playing in the huge plastic tunnels and opening their presents, as they did. Then, I turned to Crystal. "Adam's birthday is only six months away. What if I buy him a drum set?"

"Don't do it. I'd probably pull my hair out." She laughed.

"You're right. Maybe water guns would be a better idea."

Steve half whispered. "Don't you tell anyone, but I already bought Adam a Slip-N-Slide!"

I grinned. "That is what every one-year-old dreams about."

✳ ✳ ✳

I always waited in the hotel lobby, until Stacy's AA meetings were over each Tuesday and Thursday night.

On Monday, Adelle returned to work, in spite of her growing tumor and chemo. "Adelle, I finally got Stacy into AA meetings."

"That's good. Now, why don't you try an Al-Anon meeting?"

"Oh, I don't have a drinking problem. Stacy does."

"Why not pay them a visit? I believe you'll learn a whole lot in there."

I was surprised at the warm welcome I received in the gay Al-Anon group. Plus, I discovered that I was an *enabler. Who knew?* I needed to work on that issue. Before long, I approached Fred D. to be my Al-Anon Sponsor. He was a *double-winner.* That meant he had successfully worked both the AA and Al-Anon programs.

My attempts to control Stacy and his drinking ceased, after I joined Al-Anon. I began to focus on my own problem of co-dependency.

Fred chaired our meeting one night. "There are *Three C's of Alcoholism. You didn't cause someone to drink. You can't control it, and you can't cure it.*"

I smiled. *That's a mouthful of reality right there.*

✳ ✳ ✳

By late June of 1988, Stacy had saved enough money to leave home. He rented an apartment with a friend named Dana. She was working in a nail salon and taking a course at a local Junior College. I would periodically call Bradley for an update on Stacy.

One day, I received good news from him. "Stacy is busy either attending AA meetings or working in a local bar."

"Is that a good idea for him to work in a bar, as he tries to stay sober?"

"I told him how proud I am of him for staying sober, while he's working there. That's a lot of temptation for a young man."

Bradley phoned me two weeks later. "Debbie, following an old pattern, Stacy has sabotaged his success before reaching the finish line. He abruptly quit his job on July Fourth, attended a late AA meeting and left with six friends in the program."

"Within two hours, they were helplessly drunk and formed a private organization, *The Cake and Eat It Too Club.* Their membership requirement was the desire to drink uncontrollably and still work the Twelve Steps. They drank and drugged non-stop for days, except to pass out. I spotted Stacy several nights later in a car with his club members. I knew he just had a major slip by their crazy behavior, but I did as AA taught me. *I let him go.* A week passed before he called me at work."

"Bradley, I finally realize I can't control my drinking. What can I do?"

"Get your ass back in an AA meeting right now. You're in the *nine month pattern* of most newcomers. The newness of the program wears off and low self-esteem and depression returns. Stacy, you haven't worked your *Fourth Step* yet."

"Oh, that inventory thing?"

"That's the *bridge burner!* You'll never get the program without working all of the steps." *Once again, I felt Bradley had saved Stacy from sinking back into the clutches of alcoholism.*

✳ ✳ ✳

Stacy came by the house six weeks later. "Mom, I know Bradley told you what happened. I was the first one in *The Cake and Eat It Too Club* to return to AA."

✳ ✳ ✳

I slipped into an eleven o'clock meeting and picked up another *desire chip.* My new sobriety date is September 17, 1988. The next day, I called Bradley. "Well, Stacy, what did you learn from your slip?"

"I know that once I start drinking, I can't stop. The Big Book is right. I have absolutely no control over alcohol."

"What else?"

"I see the insanity of taking that first drink."

"Stacy, I won't sponsor someone who won't help their self. I want you to attend 90 meetings in 90 days and call me *every day.* Otherwise, you're wasting my time as a Sponsor."

✳ ✳ ✳

I looked at Stacy. "Is that what you're doing?"

"Yes, I'm doing it for me. I don't ever want to go back out. Also, I finally returned that historical sign from Red Rock River Park that I stole. It was part of my amends."

I teared up. "Thank goodness. I'm so proud of you for returning that sign and resuming your AA journey. I couldn't stand to lose you. *I believe that AA is actually Tough Love for Alcoholics. Truly, there are Angels among us, and Bradley is one of them.*

✳ ✳ ✳

Crystal dropped by a month later, unexpectedly. "Mom, Steve and I are going on a trip for a week. Oscar is going to keep Daniel. Can you take care of Wayne and Adam?"

"Honey, I'd love to, but my work hours aren't compatible with finding a babysitter, and I actually can't afford to hire one."

"That's okay. I just thought I'd ask."

"I have some good news about Stacy. He's now in a gay AA group called Lambda, and he has a great Sponsor named Bradley."

"You mean they actually have AA for gays?"

"Of course, they do. Why wouldn't they?"

"Oh, I don't know. He doesn't have to be gay. He chose it."

"What are you talking about? He doesn't have a choice."

"Sure he does. Gays can be changed."

"No, they can't. I didn't put in an order for a gay or straight child. I accepted him the way he arrived. He's your brother. That should be all that matters to you."

"I still think he has a choice."

"Avoiding him is not the best answer, and it can't change who he is. He's gay! Why can't you accept the truth?"

She stood up. "I've got to go." She left in a huff.

✳ ✳ ✳

I worked my Fourth Step in Al-Anon about a month after Stacy worked his with Bradley. It was a month later when Fred D. and I stopped to visit, after one of our Al-Anon meetings.

"Debbie, I think you have made great headway, but from listening to the details of your life, I believe a Pia Mellody trained psychotherapist can do more for you than an Al-Anon meeting, or I can, to deal with your past family issues."

"Where do I find such a person locally?"

"I believe when we search, the right person will appear."

✺ ✺ ✺

On January 16, 1989, Dr. K. discovered that I had massive tumors in my stomach. He and an urologist, I'd never met, performed a hysterectomy on me in the local hospital. I will never forget when I woke up in my room an hour after surgery. Dr. K. was beside my bed. I was groggy. "How did it go?"

"Everything went fine, except that we couldn't remove a sliver of ovary embedded in the lining of your stomach."

"Will that be a problem for me?"

"Not at all."

"When you go home from the hospital, come by my office, and I will show you the pictures of your tumors. They were fibroid tumors and not cancerous."

I fell asleep after he left. The next day, Dr. A., the urologist, came to see me. "Lady, you are one *Red Herring!*"

"What does that mean?"

"Your tumors were so huge that I photographed them. They should be in the Guinness World Book of Records."

My stay in the hospital wasn't dull. On day two, Stacy came by to visit, and he brought me flowers. The following day, Crystal phoned me to see how surgery went. Two hours later, a stranger entered my room. "Hi, I'm Preacher Phillips. Your daughter sent me here to visit with you." He handed me some church brochures. "Crystal wants me to talk to you about God, family, and your son."

"Excuse me?" I looked at one of his brochures. He was from *The Church on the Rock.* I returned his brochures. "Get out of my room, before I have you escorted out!"

When Stacy dropped by later, I told him about my unwanted visitor. "I can't believe Crystal sent a Preacher from her crazy church to lecture me on splitting up families again. I told him to get out." *I didn't have the heart to mention to Stacy the part about how that preacher had listed my son as a separate issue.*

✳ ✳ ✳

Mother drove me home from the hospital and got me settled. Then, she went to the grocery store and bought me some food, milk and soda pop for my refrigerator. She stayed a week, to be sure I could move around on my own, before she drove back home.

When Crystal rang my doorbell two weeks later, I was asleep on the couch. I let her inside and returned to the couch. She sat down in a chair and announced, "Mom, I want to meet my dad."

I was stunned. "After twenty-eight years, you want to meet him?"

"That's right."

"Let me remind you, he isn't a nice person, but I had to meet my dad once to see if he was as bad as Mother told me he was. I guess it's your time to learn the truth about *your dad.*"

"Then, you'll find him for me?"

"Of course, I will. Every child has a right to know *who their father is*, even if he isn't a nice person. I don't need to remind you about what he did to me."

Crystal shrugged. "Call me when you know something."

Since I'm not one who delays the inevitable, I dialed the Operator, asked for my cousin's phone number in Utah and called him. "Hey cousin, do you still work in law enforcement?"

"I do. Why do you ask?"

"Crystal wants to meet her dad after twenty-eight years."

"All I need is his full name and date of birth." I quickly rattled off the required info.

He replied, "I will call you back shortly."

In one hour, he phoned me with Jack's phone number and home address. I thanked him, hung up and dialed the number. The phone rang and rang, until a female answered. "Hi, is this the residence of Jack Harmon?"

"Yes, it is. Who is this?"

"I'm his ex-wife, Debbie."

"You have the wrong number. *Jack's only been married once.*"

"Is that what he told you? He's never been married before?"

"Seriously, I'm certain you have the wrong number."

"Did he serve in the Air Force? Is his Mother named Helen? Is his Dad named Jeff? Does he have a younger brother, Curtis, a sister Shirley, and another sister named Darlene?"

The phone went silent for several moments. Then, I heard her say in a weak voice, "We've been separated for several months."

"Has he ever hit you or tried to kill you?"

"Yes, and he is also an alcoholic."

"He learned the violence from his father who beat him and his mother. Do you have any children?"

"A beautiful daughter named Laura. He's never hurt her."

"That's good, since six of the eight times he tried to kill me, I was pregnant with our daughter, Crystal. Can she call you to ask questions about Jack?"

"That will be okay with me. My name is Norma."

"Thank you, Norma." I hung up, called Crystal, told her what I had learned, gave her Norma's number, wished her well and hung up. *Just how many times does it require that I must be a stubborn bitch to keep my head above the Churning Waters of Life?*

7

≈

Lies vs. Truth

It was a week later, when Crystal dropped by to visit and give me an update. "Mom, Norma did her best to talk me out of seeing my dad. She believes I will regret it, but I told her I want to meet him anyway."

"She gave you good advice. I do understand how you have this great need to meet him."

"At first, he told his wife that he didn't want to talk to me. A few days later, *he actually phoned me.*"

"How did it go?"

"I invited him to fly here to meet me and my family."

"He's bringing pictures. I have a half-sister named Laura. He says she's beautiful."

"Honey, I love my half-brother, so I hope you and Laura will become as close as we are."

Crystal left on *Cloud Nine.*

✳ ✳ ✳

When I was able to drive again after my surgery, I drove to Crystal and Steve's house with a birthday present for Adam. It was February 7, 1989, his first birthday. When I walked in, he was playing with a xylophone. "I thought you didn't want the kids to have anything noisy in the house."

"Mother, it's a gift from a close friend who dropped by yesterday. Adam loves it, so he gets to keep it."

I laughed. "Guess that means I can buy him a drum set next year."

"Don't you dare, I need my sanity."

✻ ✻ ✻

After I left Crystal's, I stopped at Adelle's house on the way home to see how she was doing. I knocked on her door and her daughter, Maggie, answered and let me inside. "How is Adelle?"

"She's not able to get out of bed. She went to work every day, until a week ago and then came home for good to die."

"Can I see her?"

"Yes, she's been asking about you and your surgery."

I will always remember that big smile on Adelle's face the moment she saw me. "Debbie, tell me about your surgery."

"There was no cancer. My tumors were fibroid and water-filled. I'm still weak, but I can drive. The doctor said no work for two more weeks." I took her frail hand and squeezed it.

She began to wheeze. "Can I get you something, Adelle?"

"Nothing. Eventually, my lungs will fill up with water, and I will drown, per my doctor."

Tears rolled down my cheeks. I bowed my head. "I'm so sorry."

"Don't be. I only lived this long, because I was determined to know that you made it through your surgery with no cancer."

I kissed her cheek and had to leave. I was crying so hard that I could barely see to drive home.

A week later, Maggie called me. "Debbie, Mom passed quietly last night. Her funeral is in two days. We want you to do her eulogy."

"No, I can't possibly do it. I'm still so weak, and I wouldn't be able to not cry. Please find someone else."

"Mom wanted you to do it, and so do I."

Over the next few days, I wrote a eulogy for my dear, longtime friend, Adelle. I vaguely remember looking out at the overflowing auditorium of her church. I had to hold onto the podium for the strength to stand. When I finished, there wasn't a dry eye to be seen, including my mine. I didn't go to the cemetery that day. It was too much for me to handle.

A week later, Stacy drove me to the cemetery. Ironically, it was the same cemetery where his high school girlfriend, Patty, was also buried after her tragic, hit-and-run death. I put flowers on Adelle's grave, and then we both put flowers on Patty's grave. Stacy wanted me to take his picture beside her tombstone. It was a difficult day for both of us.

✱ ✱ ✱

On April first, Crystal phoned one weekend. "Mom, Dad's here. I'm planning a family dinner tomorrow, and I want you to come."

"Excuse me? You can't seriously expect me to sit down for a meal with the man who tried to kill me *eight times*. I'm not going to be there. Crystal, *I found him for you, not for me.*"

"I thought you might want to see him. He wants to see you."

"No, thank you!" *My disappointment with Crystal and her insensitive request cut me to the quick. Only because of my Guardian Angels are either one of us still alive today, in spite of this abusive monster. She has no idea of the terror I went through to keep us alive.*

✱ ✱ ✱

Two weeks later, at midnight, I was awakened by the nonstop ringing of my doorbell. I walked to the door, looked thru the peephole and opened the door. "Stacy, this is a surprise."

"Can I talk to you, Mom?"

"Sure, what's the matter? Are you okay?"

He hurried past me with tear-filled eyes. He almost dove onto the den sofa. Eons seemed to pass, so I spoke first. "Honey, tell me what's wrong, so I can help you." He burst out crying. I put my arm around his shoulder.

"I think I'm a *Love Addict*."

"Tell me what happened."

I sat patiently and listened to my son explain about a guy who liked him, but he didn't feel the same way. Then, he met a guy he liked who didn't have those feelings for him. Now, he's depressed and suicidal.

"Mom, a *Voice of Intuition* insisted that my answer was somehow with you."

"Sweetie, it's time I told you about my struggle with Love Addiction. I met Dan twenty-three years ago at work. He kept chasing after me and wouldn't stop. He promised to leave his wife, and swore he loved me so much. For several months, we had an affair. Eventually, I couldn't take the guilt anymore. I wrote his wife a letter, apologized for our brief affair, mailed it to her, quit my job and moved to Tennessee."

"That's where I met your dad, Tim, after I got a job at a telephone company. I was attracted to his emotional unavailability without knowing it. Actually, my heart was hurting. I had just broken it off with Dan, and I loved him so much. One day, he even mailed me a wedding ring and wrote me that if I would call him, we'd get married. I never made that call. I promised myself that I'd *never* let that happen to me again, *and I haven't*. I doubt I would have married Tim, had it not been for Dan, but then, I wouldn't have you."

"Now I know why I had an urgent need to see you, Mom. Unexplainably, I somehow knew my answer was *written in your heart*, and I had to see you right away. On the way here, I had thoughts of driving my car under a semi-truck to end it all, but an equally defying *Voice of Reason* kept insisting, 'The answer to your pain is with your mother. Wait for it!'"

"Stacy, you get into sick relationships exactly like I have done. Those two boys were a means to resolve an old issue."

"There's one question that I must ask you, Mom."

"Ask me anything. I'll tell you the truth, no matter how painful the answer. *I believe truth holds the power of healing.*"

"How did I come to be?"

"By the time I discovered that Tim was an alcoholic, I was pregnant with you. When he told me he didn't want to marry me, I wanted you anyway.

Tim's mother, Dana, cornered him. "Son, you will marry Debbie. She's carrying your child, my grandchild, and I want to be a grandmother"

"Was my birth the reason your marriage didn't work and why you eventually divorced him?"

"Of course not. I doubt I ever loved Tim. I chased after his unavailability, to continue living as a Love Addict. Honey, we both love you very much. The failure of our marriage had nothing to do with your birth. It would have failed anyway because of his serious drinking, even if I did love him."

✳ ✳ ✳

Years later, Stacy told me that at that moment he experienced an overwhelming *Feeling of Spirituality*. "It was as if a burning sensation entered my upper chest near the center of my body and below my neck. I sensed that the spot, where I'd always felt a giant void of emptiness, was suddenly filling up."

"I am so glad you asked me instead of hurting yourself."

"Since that morning, I've never felt empty again. For weeks, even months afterward, I feared the feeling would leave, and I would once again feel empty and hopeless. Happily, that has never happened. My talk with you was the beginning of my true spiritual experience in AA. Only after that night did I stop my denial and honestly begin working the AA program."

I smiled at Stacy. "Tonight you hit an emotional bottom, but *an old would was healed by the truth.*"

✳ ✳ ✳

After an Al-Anon meeting a month later, Fred D. stopped me in the hall. "Great news, I have finally met a Pia Mellody-trained psychotherapist for you." He handed me a card for Betty T.

I phoned her from work the next day and made an appointment. "I have no openings until May 25th at nine a.m."

✳ ✳ ✳

The next day was May 24, 1989. I was eager to see Betty the next day. As I entered my work building, I approached Johnny. He was getting a cup of coffee in the lunchroom and smiled. "How are you today?"

"I feel on top of the world."

"About something good, I hope?"

"Yes, I believe it will be very beneficial to me. I'm going to see a psychotherapist to work out some old family issues."

"I'm glad to hear it."

We entered our work area together and went our separate ways. Later that afternoon, I was standing up talking to Lori. Suddenly, I felt a sharp pain in my lower back. I dismissed it, but the pain soon began to move. It slowly crept around my right side and stopped just past my right hip. Instantly, I knew I needed surgery. I slowly ambled to a phone on a nearby post. I called Dr. K's office, told his nurse about my agonizing pain and that I was on my way there. I found Ivan. "I need to see my doctor. I have a horrible pain in my right side."

"Okay. When will you be back?"

What did he just ask me? "This could be my appendix, so I'm not sure when I'll be back." *Ivan the Terrible strikes again! I feel like I'm dying and this selfish man can only think about himself, the job and to Hell with me and my excruciating pain.*

I slowly gathered my things and made it outside to my car. It felt like forever, before I finally arrived at Dr. K's office only ten minutes away. His nurse made me wait, until she realized I was doubled over in pain. She put me in a patient room. By then, tears were pouring down my cheeks from the horrific pain.

Finally, Dr. K. came in, examined me and pushed on my side. I almost came off the table. "I think it's nothing serious. I'm going to write you a prescription." *Nothing serious? Surely I didn't hear this maniac right! He hasn't even run a test on me.*

"Is that a prescription for my unbearable pain?"

"It will take care of your problem." He handed me my prescription. "Come back in the morning, if you aren't any better."

Slowly, I managed to make it to my car and drive to a pharmacy. I handed my prescription to the Pharmacist. He frowned.

"What kind of prescription did he give me for my pain?"

"This is for male hormones."

"Oh no, that must be a mistake. I need something for the excruciating pain in my side."

"I'll call Dr. K. to confirm this for you." He went to his phone and quickly returned. "This is correct, per his nurse."

"Okay." I sat in a nearby chair until my prescription was filled and slowly drove home. Once inside my door, I could barely walk for the sharp pain. I took a male hormone and reclined on my couch. *I doubted my ability to survive the next hour, much less live through a full night.*

✳ ✳ ✳

During the night, my pain rose in intensity. I felt as if I was about to die. I couldn't sleep for my horrendous side pain. *I have no idea how I lived through that awful night, except that Angels must have watched over me to keep me alive.* It is the worst physical pain I have ever endured in my whole life.

At eight a.m., I managed to get to my bedroom, pack a gown and makeup in a small bag, grab my pillow and slowly make it to my car. *Again, I have no explanation of how I drove anywhere that morning, other than my Angels drove my car.*

When I arrived at Dr. K's office, I looked at his nurse. *"I need surgery."*

"Oh God, you're white as a ghost! I'll get you to a room."

I wasn't able to get on the exam table. I remained slumped over in a chair hugging my pillow. When Dr. K. walked in, my weak voice uttered, *"Get me to a hospital."*

The next thing I knew, I was on a cold, steel table with bright lights above me. "Where am I?"

A Lab Technician answered. "We just shot you full of red dye. I can see why you're in so much pain."

"So, why am I?"

"There's a huge ball of something that's blocked your kidneys."

The next thing I recall, I was being wheeled into a surgery room. Dr. K. and Dr. A. were beside me. Dr. K. explained, "We're going to do an Endoscopic Retrograde on you, so we can look inside and see what's happening."

When I woke up in my hospital room, my throat was so sore I couldn't speak. Both doctors came in to see me. Dr. A. smiled. *"You're in good hands.* We are going to operate tomorrow and stop your pain. For now, you're on small doses of our strongest painkiller."

After they left, Mother and Lori came into my room. I couldn't talk, but I could write notes. Mother held my hand. "We'll be here in the morning while they operate. I'll take care of you when you get released."

I nodded and soon fell asleep. The next morning, I vaguely recall being wheeled into surgery. Afterward, I eventually woke up. Mother and Lori were standing beside my bed. Neither one of them looked very happy. "What's wrong?"

Lori hesitated. "You aren't going to believe what they did. Only one of the doctors came out and talked to us. Dr. A. explained that they opened you up, slit a huge, water-filled tumor open and sutured it back into the lining of your stomach."

"What were those idiots thinking?" *There is a special place in Hell for doctors like these two yo-yo's.*

✳✳✳

My doctors kept me in the hospital for twelve long days. During that time, I asked Dr. A., "Why the delay in allowing me to go home?"

"You must have been in some tremendous pain. Debbie, your body somehow tied your catheter tube into three knots. I've never seen anything like it." *No kidding, doc!*

"I told Dr. K. I needed surgery the day I walked into his office, and he sent me home with male hormones."

Dr. A. ignored my comment and left my room. When I was finally released, Mother drove me home and stayed for several days. I phoned Betty T. and explained why I missed my first appointment.

"I completely understand, Debbie. I have an opening a week from Monday at nine a.m."

"I'll be there."

That Monday, Mother drove me to Betty's office and waited in her lobby, while I met Betty. Oddly, Betty and I resembled each other in size and color of hair. I found her easy to talk with and a good listener. I gave her an overview of my past and added, "I'm here to work on my biggest problem."

She chuckled. "And what would that be?"

"I'm a Love Addict."

"Yes, you are, but I think you have several other issues we will need to address before we're through. It appears that *all your life, you have been attracted to dysfunctional men who were emotionally unavailable and unable to love anyone.*"

Soon, my hour ended. When I stood up to leave, Betty gave me a warm hug. I felt relief, and somehow knew, that Fred D. had found the right person for me to work with me on my issues.

✱ ✱ ✱

Crystal phoned me two weeks later. "Mom, someone wants to meet you. Can we come over?"

"Not if it's your dad, Jack."

"It's my half-sister, Laura. We look so much alike!"

"Sure, I'd love to meet her."

"We'll be there in an hour."

The hour passed quickly. Crystal knocked on my door. I let her and Laura inside. Crystal was right. Laura looked a lot like her, and she was just as pretty.

I hugged her. "I'm glad to meet you. You're beautiful."

She blushed. "And to think, I had no idea Dad had ever been married before, and you two had Crystal. She's the sister I've always wanted."

"Mom, we want a couple of pictures together. Do you mind?"

"Of course I don't." I retrieved my camera and took several photos. "I'll get extra prints made. Crystal can mail you copies."

"That would be lovely, Debbie."

We chatted for about an hour, and then they left so Crystal could take Laura sight-seeing. I walked them to Crystal's car and saw my mailman walk onto my porch. When I turned around, he was waiting with a package for me. I thanked him and went inside to open a large manila envelope. I never expected to see what I was about to find inside that package.

There was a short note from my brother, Matt, written on a notepad. *"Debbie, maybe you have this, but if you don't, I hope it helps you as much as it has helped me. Love you, Matt."*

I hurriedly removed a large object wrapped in newspaper. Matt had sent me a *Footprints* plaque. I was moved to tears. My brother had never once talked about God, belief or faith to me.

✳ ✳ ✳

Stacy and I had lunch a month later. We had just attended a Pia Mellody Workshop together two weeks before that. He wanted to tell me how listening to Pia had changed his life.

✳ ✳ ✳

It took six long hours, but I completed my *Fifth Step. I admitted to God, to myself and to another human my wrongs.* Then, Bradley stood up, opened his arms wide and gave me a big hug. Relief swirled around me when I realized he still liked me, in spite of my many mistakes.

"Now, Stacy, I'll make it easy for you. I made a list of people you need to make amends to for your *Eighth Step. Made a list of all persons I've harmed and made amends to them."*

I patiently waited while Bradley wrote out my list, folded it up and handed it to me.

"Put this list in your pocket. Don't read it until you do Steps Six and Seven. Go straight home, do the steps and then read the list."

Bradley lived only three blocks from my apartment, so I walked home and sat in Janet's antique barber chair in my living room with the *Big Book* resting in my lap. I read Steps Six and Seven aloud. *"Was ready for God to remove my character defects and humbly asked that He remove them."*

As I closed my eyes, I prayed aloud, "God, I'm finally ready to let you remove my character defects and please, remove my shortcomings, too."

A spiritual feeling permeated the room. I pulled Bradley's list from my shirt pocket to read the list of people I'd hurt the most. To my great shock, the first name on the list was *Stacy Malone.* Bradley forced me to see that, of all the people in my life, I'd hurt myself the most. I simply couldn't believe it. My second shock was that the list was so short. I did all of my amends within months. Dad was the hardest, because I'd lied to him a lot. After I finished making my amends to him, I waited for his response.

"I'm a little stunned, but I love you. I'm glad you're doing better."

He finally managed to mumble unfamiliar words.

"You're the most important person in my life."

It was during this time, when you began seeing your psychotherapist, Betty T., and bought those Pia Melody tapes on religious addiction, love addiction, and co-dependency. After you heard about my attachment to Darrin, you insisted I listen to Pia's tapes on *Love Addiction.* Instantly, I related to her explanation of a boundary-less need for love from another person. When I told Bradley that I was a Love Addict, he disagreed and wanted me to stay with the AA philosophy. "Stay away from that mush." Yet my heart insisted I continue, since I knew I had to deal with other issues, or I'd go back out and find a way to medicate them.

✳ ✳ ✳

Three weeks later, I went out to coffee with my Al-Anon group. As we were leaving, Stacy walked in with several of his AA friends.

Here is what he was eventually able to tell me six weeks later.

✳ ✳ ✳

After you left, I stayed there another two hours with my friends. Even in AA, there are clicks, ego trips, and sick people. Mickey O. felt like he and a small group ran the eleven p.m. AA meeting. Apparently, there was a lot of jealousy over my recent success in AA. They were hoping I'd slip and go back out.

Due to my exposure to Pia Melody's teachings, I was feeling spiritual and spoke out a lot in meetings. Mickey O. resented my remarks. He believed he was the late-night guru. He wanted me out of AA. It was an obvious *power play.* I recall that Mickey sat next to me that night.

"Stacy, you have no idea how the AA journey works, but you will find out real soon."

Since I had become a leader instead of a follower, Mickey felt threatened. As with most control-freaks, he was pissed off. I listened to my own drummer. I knew I had learned helpful things they didn't teach yet in AA. I'd grown past them spiritually. Unfortunately, the *know-it-all* process is necessary in recovery, and Mickey's was the worst case I'd ever seen.

He continued messing with my head that night with his obnoxious remarks. I vaguely remember feeling strange before I left the coffee shop. By the time I walked home to my apartment, I was extremely queasy. Everything was out of dimension, just like the PCP experience I'd had at home with Patty years ago.

When I opened my apartment door, walls leaned way back or came toward me. Distorted dimension was everywhere. Even Hummer, my kitty, looked like a giant lion crossing my hardwood floor. The only difference between this time and the one many years ago was that this one was totally mental. I turned off the lights, and I wondered if it was a PCP flashback or an oddity, since I'd just quit smoking. For a while, I stayed on my bed. It felt like everything was closing in on me and would eventually smash me to bits. I feared turning on lights. I didn't want to see any more moving walls.

Just then, my phone rang. "Are you okay?"

"Who is this?"

"Jeff M., I was sitting beside you at coffee tonight. You were acting funny when you left the coffee shop."

"Why did you call me?"

"Do you want to drive to my apartment?"

"Okay."

I agreed, since I was still unsure of what was wrong with me, and I feared being alone. The four block drive to Jeff's was strange, yet somehow I made it. I desperately wanted out of my apartment, for fear I was going crazy.

During the next four hours, we talked about God and spirituality.

"Stacy, it looks to me like you've had an unusual spiritual experience. Sort of like a *burning bush* encounter or something."

After I stayed up all night at Jeff's, I felt okay and returned home. When I entered my apartment, exhaustion consumed me in a deep sleep. The next day, I woke up feeling alone, confused, and lost. I didn't go to work, closed all my blinds and began to have grandiose illusions about the end of the world.

My upstairs AA neighbor, Sam, knocked on my door. I let him inside. He used my phone and called Bradley. "Stacy's messed up bad. Come over here, quick!"

Bradley arrived shortly. He and Sam helped me into Bradley's Cadillac. He drove me to his condo. I was still unsure what was wrong with me or what to do. By that time, I was unable to talk sensibly. My mind reasoned; *I must be talking in tongues.*

A frantic Bradley phoned Tim. "Stacy's incoherent. You'd better come over here quick and take him to a hospital!"

When Dad arrived, *he drove me to his apartment instead of to a hospital* over Bradley's loud objections. Dad's reaction wasn't surprising. He never could make important decisions. Luckily for me, Bradley called you at work.

"Debbie, there's something drastically wrong with Stacy. He's like a robot. I can't talk to him. When I called Tim to take him to a hospital, he came and took him home instead. You'd better go check on him." *Leave it to my indecisive dad to avoid making a decision to take care of his own son. He'll never change!*

You begged off work and drove to Dad's apartment. Even today, I remember watching you kneel on the floor to listen to me speak in some strange tongue. All I could do was move rigidly like a space robot. My eyes could only stare at an invisible space in front of me, as if they were frozen. It was like an invisible force had captured my undivided attention. Oddly, I could hear you and Dad talking, but I was completely unable to converse with you.

In minutes, I saw you burst into tears. *"Stacy's a vegetable!"*

You never hesitated and turned to Dad. "Help me load Stacy into my car. Why didn't you take him to the hospital, instead of bringing him here? He needs help!"

Per Dad's usual, he gave you no reply. He just shrugged his shoulders. Once I was safely strapped into your front bucket seat, you took off for Freeman Hospital's Emergency Room and arrived in record time. You led me toward a glassed-in nurse's area. Several nurses took one look at me and helped me onto a gurney in the hallway. The Head Nurse didn't look up. "We're so busy right now. We don't have even one empty room, Mrs. Malone."

✳ ✳ ✳

Stacy, that's when I went into sheer panic mode. "I'm Ms. Austin, and my son needs a doctor right away!"

She gently patted my arm. "We'll call Dr. Nightingale right now. He specializes in these kinds of cases."

"What kinds of cases? How do you know what's wrong with Stacy? You haven't even tested him yet!"

"We've seen this behavior type before." You began to mumble incoherently again, as two male interns showed up and strapped you to a gurney.

Tears rolled down my cheeks, *as I watched you cry out like a mongoloid in dreadful pain. Then, they rolled you away.*

8

≈

Nightmare Alley

The Head Nurse insisted I wait in the front hallway, until Dr. Nightingale arrived. I went to squeeze Stacy's hand, before I walked to the front. *This is a friggin' nightmare!*

The wait for Dr. Nightingale seemed endless. An hour later, he and his young assistant arrived to examine Stacy. When I saw Dr. Nightingale, he reminded me of a *Mad Scientist* complete with a gray goatee and half-moon glasses. The two of them visited briefly with me in a cracker box-sized room.

"Ms. Austin, I am going to order numerous tests be run on Stacy. The worst one will be a spinal tap." I stepped into the hallway, as two orderlies wheeled him into a nearby room. My heart broke the moment I heard him screaming in horrible pain from the spinal tap.

Finally, the Head Nurse allowed me to visit Stacy again. "Dr. Nightingale wants to discuss your son's test results with you." She turned to Stacy. "One of your AA friends is here to see you. His name is Jeff M."

Stacy still couldn't talk, but he furiously shook his head, "No!"

I looked at him. "You don't want to see Jeff?" He gave me the same response that he gave the Head Nurse. Next, she led me into a small examining room to see Dr. Nightingale and his young assistant. I sat down.

"I'm sorry, Ms. Austin. We think Stacy has dementia."

"Never heard of it. What does that mean?"

"Well, someone could have given him an unknown drug that fractured his mind."

"Can't it wear off?"

"Not necessarily, if that's what happened. There's no trace of drugs in his system, and there is no detectable disease like AIDS, so clinically, I must diagnose him as *crazy!*"

"I'll never believe that! I'll find a way to stop you!"

"We must ship him to Russell State Mental Hospital."

"Not without a second opinion you won't!"

"Very well, but prepare yourself for the worst."

"My son isn't going to Russell." I fled the room, stopped to talk to Stacy and hoped he could understand me. I rushed to a hallway pay phone and frantically called my Sponsor, Fred D. I told him about my dilemma. Next, I phoned Bradley. After I hung up, I tried to check Stacy out of the hospital. The nurses had orders not to release him. By that time it was four a.m.

I drove home to get some sleep and planned to get back on the telephone by eight a.m. *I must find a deliverer for my son.* Instead, I returned to the hospital at seven a.m.

In AA and Al-Anon, miracles continually happen. Word of my problem had spread through Lambda like wildfire. When I parked my car, Martin C., an anesthesiologist at Freeman Hospital, and also a member of Lambda's AA program, appeared by my side in his white doctor's smock. We turned to see two nurses rolling Stacy toward an ambulance.

✳ ✳ ✳

A month later, Stacy was able to tell me what he was feeling at that exact frightening moment.

✳ ✳ ✳

My eyes were barely able to focus on Martin's strikingly handsome face. At first, I thought I was dying, and he was my Guardian Angel sent by God to take me across the portal called *death*. I could hear voices arguing over my head. It was Martin.

"No, he's my patient. He's not going to Russell. I want him released to my care right now!"

The trembling nurse objected. "He can't leave, until I speak to Dr. Nightingale."

She rushed back inside the hospital. Martin lifted me upward and removed my restraints. "Come on, Stacy, we're getting you out of here!"

I heard the other nurse yell. "That young man is crazy. He can't leave with you!"

"Step out of my way. He's my patient, not yours!" Martin grabbed my chart, scanned the list of medications I'd received since I had arrived at the hospital and shouted, "He's almost a vegetable now. Look at all of the medications you've given him so far!"

He threw his sport jacket around my shoulders and helped me into his red Corvette parked near the emergency door and sped away.

The next day, he called you, Mom. "Stacy's at my home across town. I plan to nurse him back to health. Call me tomorrow, and I'll tell you when he can be moved."

When you phoned Martin, I heard him talking to you. "You can pick Stacy up tomorrow. He's getting some of his strength and color back. Someone gave him an untraceable, mind-altering drug. From what I've learned from Jeff M., Mickey O. works in a psychiatric ward for the terminally insane. He cares for people who've overdosed on drugs and fried their brain. He could be *the culprit.* Even in AA, there's no guarantee of sanity in others."

✳ ✳ ✳

Stacy, after I hung up the phone from talking with Martin, sheer exhaustion carried me to the couch. I slept for twelve hours.

When I arrived at his home the next day, a friend of yours I hadn't met yet, named Richard H., arrived. He and Martin put you into his car. I patted your hand. "This has been like a *Nightmare from Hell* for me, honey."

Richard H. drove you to your apartment. I followed in my car. Your kitty, Hummer, met you at your apartment door. I watched you stretch out on your half-bed. Hummer fell asleep by your side. I was stunned at how weak you still were. It appeared as if every ounce of energy had been sucked from your veins by a giant straw. I finally had to leave for work. Richard slept on your couch to watch over you.

Two days later, you left me a phone message."

"Mom, I returned to my telemarketing job at Divine Energy today. My boss is Joseph G. He's also in AA."

It was the first I had heard about your job and Joseph G. I was thrilled that you were healthy and functioning again, instead of being locked up in an insane asylum as a crazy person.

✳ ✳ ✳

That weekend, I phoned Crystal and told her about what had happened to Stacy. "So, how are things in your world, Crystal?"

"Good actually."

"I'd like to buy you lunch tomorrow at Red Lobster."

"Sounds good, Mom."

The next day, we enjoyed our meal, and I looked at Crystal. "Honey, you may not know it, but I'm in Al-Anon. I have a gay sponsor and recently worked my *Fourth Step* with him."

"What does that mean?"

"It means that I made *an inventory of myself* and did the *Eighth Step. Made a list of persons I had harmed and willingly made amends to them.*"

Crystal got an uncomfortable look on her face.

"When you asked me to visit you at that church, and you held Adam on your lap, you stated that I wasn't a good Mother to you, and I didn't touch you. I'm sorry you feel that way. It isn't that I don't love you. I gave you a whole lot more love and touching than I ever received from Mother. I want you to know I did the best I could, considering what I was given by my parents. I plan to do much better in the future, but I can't unring a bell of the past."

Crystal thought about it for a long time. "Thank you for saying that. It means a lot to me." Then, she added, "Mom, you're going to be a grandmother again in February."

"That's great. Maybe we'll get a little girl this time."

"I hope so!"

We stood up to leave, and I gave Crystal a warm hug. "I love you so much, honey!"

"I love you, too!"

✳ ✳ ✳

It seemed that my family was now on a healthier path. At work, my co-workers decided that I would make a good representative to deal with our boss, Ivan Stone. I'm not sure how they arrived at that decision, since he and I weren't exactly good friends.

In no time flat, Ivan's night assistant, Chase Smart, fired an older man we'd nicknamed *Spare Wheel* for stealing trash. I had to meet with the company Production Manager, Allen Cole, and Chase Smart in an attempt to save Spare Wheel's job.

When Spare Wheel and I met in the Conference Room with them, I began. "I've never heard of anyone being fired for stealing trash. Where do you have that posted in the Company Rules?"

Production Manager Allen turned to Chase for a reply. Chase took over. "Stealing is an offense for firing."

"In your judgment or in the company's posted rules? We are talking about a box of trash."

"It had a handwritten sign on top of it. *Do not remove.*

"Spare Wheel, did you see a sign on top of that box?"

"Not at first. It showed up later in the day, after Chase got mad at me for being two minutes late returning from supper."

I stared at Chase and leaned forward. "What if I have a witness *who saw* the person put that handwritten sign on top of that trash box? And what if that person is sitting in this very room? It wouldn't look good on someone's resume, now would it?"

Instantly, Chase's face flushed blood red. I knew he wasn't telling the truth. He didn't know if I was or not.

Production Manager Allen finally spoke up. "If that box of trash is returned to us, we will consider the case closed."

✶ ✶ ✶

Two weeks later on a Friday afternoon, Stacy dropped by the house for a visit before I left for work. He sat down with a worried look.

"Mom, Joseph G. called all of his Management Assistants into his office an hour ago and made an announcement. 'All of you have done a good job. I think you should know, I just sold the company to Andy R.' All of us reeled in shock, as we watched him clean out his desk, shake our hands and leave."

"Honestly, I couldn't blame Joseph for selling the company. It was two-hundred-thousand-dollars in debt, and the ground leases were out of oil, so he settled for eight-thousand-dollars from Andy's pocketbook."

"I gathered my few things and headed here with my sanity in one hand and the *Serenity Prayer* in the other. I prayed, *God, grant me serenity to accept things I can't change, courage to change what*

I can, and wisdom to understand the difference. Then, I rode here on my moped. Can I use your phone?"

"Of course you can."

I listened, as he called Tim at his Suburban Weekly Newspaper. "Dad, I need a job. Can I come work for you at your paper?"

I smiled. *I knew Tim would give Stacy a job.*

✳ ✳ ✳

On July 16, 1989, I finally had my first visit with Betty T. "Debbie, I want you to go way back and tell me your childhood memories."

Once I finished telling her about my life up to age 13, Betty held up her hand. "It sounds like you had a childhood void caused by *minimal nurturing* from parents who were immature and came from a dysfunctional family system themselves. Your mother and father certainly had no parenting skills, nor did your step-dad. They were mostly interested in getting their own needs met, rather than meeting those of a lonely little girl named Debbie."

As I listened to her assessment, I grew overly sad and withdrawn.

"How does that make you feel, Debbie?"

I heaved a big sigh. "Like I need to cry for me."

"I am going to take you into *the dark forest of your past.* There will come a day when I will lead you out of that dark forest, but first, we have a lot of work to do. I want you to reach out and touch at least five people in the next week. I am giving you permission to do this. It is what people who have been raised in a healthy family learn from healthy parents."

"I don't know if I can do it. It feels strange to me, when I touch other people. It always has."

"We are going to change that."

✳ ✳ ✳

I made myself touch five people during the next few days. I could only bring myself to touch one person a day. I was surprised each time I did it, especially when no one reacted negatively.

Ten days passed, and a familiar pain returned in my right side. I phoned Dr. K.'s office and made an appointment to see my photos that Dr. A. had taken of my enormous tumors.

After I arrived, I approached his nurse. She hassled me. "Ms. Austin, you have an outstanding balance from your surgery."

"No Ma'am, I mailed you a check two weeks ago."

She opened her ledger and found that she had posted it on the tenth of the month. She didn't bother to apologize. His nurse weighed me in and I explained, "I'm not here on an office call. I came to see pictures of my surgery tumors."

She gritted her teeth and led me into Dr. K.'s office. After I sat down, he showed me six pictures of my tumors. "Will the tumors or my endometriosis ever return?"

His answer was curt. "No!"

"I've had a pain in my right side since last Friday. You told me that might happen. Will it go away?"

"You're *probably not actually having a pain.* It must be your imagination." *My brief time with Betty T. had taught me that Dr. K. was denying my feeling reality about having pain again.*

"Dr. K., you told me that I might have this pain."

A second time he denied his own words. "I never told you that." Then, he snapped at me. "This isn't an office visit. You need to make an appointment to have that discussion."

I stood up. "You're right!"

Before I could turn to leave, he ordered, "And, shut the door on your way out!"

When I opened his door, I slammed it shut as I left.

*** * ***

At work the next day, I approached Lori. "Will you help me plan a Baby Shower for Crystal?"

"Sure and you can even have it at my house."

"That's perfect. I'll let Crystal know."

After I notified Crystal and Mother about the upcoming Baby Shower, I decided to make something special for her baby gift. I spent weeks making a pink-and-blue macramé hanger with big plastic baby rattlers, bows as decorations and a piece of round glass to make it a hanging table. I wanted to surprise Crystal with it.

The day of Crystal's shower, Mother arrived at my home first. I showed her the macramé hanging table. "I plan to surprise Crystal, so I'm going to hide it in my car trunk."

Crystal drove up just as I closed my trunk. They rode with me to Lori's house. Mother sat in my front seat. Crystal was in the back seat, when Mother blurted out, "Oh Crystal, wait until you see the macramé hanger your mom made for your shower gift."

I couldn't believe what Mother just did. "There went my big surprise, Mother. Thank you very much!"

She flashed her familiar wounded expression at me, once again. It was as if what she had just said was entirely my fault.

✳ ✳ ✳

Two weeks passed. I phoned Stacy at Tim's newspaper. "Hi, how about I buy you supper after you get off work tomorrow?"

"Sounds good."

Later, I met Stacy at his favorite restaurant, *Moonshine Patio Bar & Grill.* We ordered our food. "How are things going at work?"

"Dad picks me up every day on his way to his newspaper. I sell ads and create advertising layouts in his grungy little office. In only a matter of days, he got mad at me. 'Stacy, I don't like your style. You lie to my advertisers to sell ads.' "

"So what! I tell one company their competitor bought a quarter page classified ad. And what are you going to buy?"

"That's dishonest, because it isn't true."

"No, Dad, it's called salesmanship. Then, I contact their competitor and tell them the same thing. So far, I've sold two ads that way."

"You can't lie to sell ads. It's unprincipled."

"I say, screw the principles. Let's make money."

"Rather than argue with me any further, he disappeared and had another drink somewhere in his back office piled high with old newspapers. Soon, he put my name on his masthead as Advertising Director; Grandmother Malone was listed as Office Secretary; Dad as Publisher. To have the entire Malone family together to run a newspaper was always Dad's lifetime dream-come-true."

"My encounter with him had made me nauseous. He's so dumb business-wise. If I made any innovative suggestions on ways to get ahead, he'd shoot down my idea. My annoyance blossomed by the hour. Two weeks ago, I stopped by Divine Energy to get my last paycheck. Their secretary called me into her office for advice."

"Tell me about Joseph G."

"What about him?"

"He called me yesterday and offered me a job."

"So?"

"The way he left here bothers me. He's sort of a crook."

"What I saw was an investment gone sour. Joseph merely cut his losses and got out. You're right, crooks are good business people. By the way, would you mind giving Joseph my phone number? Even though he could be a crook, I need a job."

I looked at Stacy. "Why would you work for Joseph again?"

"It beats waiting tables, and I need to get away from Dad. His negative attitude and drinking are hazardous to my recovery process. Three hours later, Joseph called me at Dad's paper."

"Why don't we meet after tonight's eight p.m. AA meeting and talk about your new job?"

✳ ✳ ✳

When my next appointment with Betty arrived, she began. "Today, we are going to do some *Shame Reduction Work*. It is symbolic work of giving back to people who have offended you."

"How do we do that?"

"All your life, your child has been in charge of you. I want you to bring yourself into this room at the age of six to ten. Have her sit in a chair and talk to you. You need to describe her to me. Does she look sad, lonely, afraid or intimidated? Tell her that she was abused, and you are now the adult who will protect her. Move her into your lap, rock her, and wrap your heart around that child to let her know that you will now start taking care of her."

After I did as Betty instructed, she cocked her head. "How old is your child?"

"My child is about five. My adult is twenty-two. My body is forty-six. What a mess I am!" Suddenly, I burst into tears.

✳ ✳ ✳

That night after I fell asleep, I awoke and wept for my inner child who had been mistreated for so many years. As I stood up, my brother called. "Sis, Mother tells me you are in psychotherapy. I want to know why you have labeled yourself as a Co-Dependent."

"My recovery process is not open for debate."

"I went through abuse from your dad, but I'm fine."

"You're deluding yourself. He physically abused you, too. You buried it and never dealt with it. I am working on my issues."

Our phone call ended on poor terms. Later at work, Lori invited me to go out for lunch. As we ate, she verbally attacked me. "Debbie, you don't need therapy. You are a much stronger person than I am. You helped me so much, when I discovered that my then husband had possibly committed incest with his sisters."

"Lori, it's time for you to visit a Recovery Group and get a Sponsor. I'm doing good work with Betty, and no one will stop me."

※ ※ ※

Yesterday proved to be a whole lot to handle when I woke up. I was thinking about Betty T. and the attacks from my brother and Lori about my recovery process. Then, my phone rang. It was Bart.

"Hi, goodlookin', how are things going?"

"I've had better days. How are you?"

"My offer of a plane ticket to fly here for a visit is still open."

"You know I can't do that. It wouldn't be good for me."

"Ah shucks, baby, there will be no strings attached. I promise I will rent you a hotel room. I just want to see you."

In a terrible moment of feeling sorry for myself over what Matt and Lori had said to me the previous day, I replied, "Okay, but no *Monkey Business.* I can only stay one night."

"I'll make your plane and hotel reservations right now."

After I hung up, I went and gazed at myself in a mirror. "Who made that decision? Was it my child or my adult? What will Betty say?" I threw caution to the wind and went into the garage to find my suitcase. It was stored in a homemade closet in the garage that Bart had built for me years ago. When I reached for the hook to unlock the closet door, suddenly a two-by-four, that was part of the door frame, fell straight down and smashed the big toe on my left foot. Blood gushed everywhere. I went into shock. It felt as if my toe was completely severed. I grew sick at my stomach and passed out.

Lucky for me, Stacy happened to drop by and rang the doorbell. He knew I should be home, since my car was parked out front. When I didn't answer, he let himself in and came looking for me. I vaguely recall seeing him open the door.

"Dear God, what happened, Mom?"

"I'm afraid to look at my toe. Is it severed?"

"I don't think so."

He almost carried me into the den to the couch, found bandages for my bleeding toe and an icepack. "What were you doing when that board fell?"

"Get me some aspirin for my pain, and I'll tell you." He found a bottle of aspirin and brought me a glass of water.

"Apparently, God wanted to get my attention and had to break my big toe almost off to stop me from visiting Bart."

"You were going to go see Bart?"

"I was. Call and tell him I can't go anywhere. I'm hurt bad." I chuckled weakly. *"Believe me, I received God's message loud and clear. No more Bart!"*

9

≈

So Many People, So Much Pain

Stacy phoned Bart, as I listened from the couch. "Mom's big toe is broken. She tried to open that big closet in the garage, and a two-by-four on the door frame fell and almost cut off her big toe. She can't fly there to see you."

"Tell her that I'm sorry to hear about her injury."

Next, Stacy phoned Crystal and told her what happened to me. By that time, I had fallen asleep. He quietly left and locked the front door.

The next day, Crystal knocked on the door. It was all I could do to hobble to the front door to let her inside. She helped me back onto the couch. Blood was seeping through my foot bandage.

"Honey, would you go to the hall bathroom and bring me more bandages and the scissors?"

Crystal returned with the items and helped me rewrap my broken toe. Then, she sat down on the other end of my couch. "Mom, I have a letter that I wrote to you."

"Oh? What's it about?"

She handed it to me. I didn't open it. I sensed it was something I didn't need to deal with, while I was in such unbearable pain.

"Aren't you going to open it?"

"Not until you tell me what it's about."

"It's about my church and how splitting families is okay."

"You know what? We've already been through this. I'm not going to read your letter. I thought we had settled this issue."

"It isn't settled, as far as I'm concerned."

"Churches do *not* split up families, and that's final."

She snatched the letter from my hand and left. I looked upward. *God, when will this insanity with Crystal ever end?*

✳ ✳ ✳

My broken toe caused me to miss two weeks from my job. I phoned Betty T. and set up an appointment on the following Friday. When I arrived, I admitted to her that I had agreed to go see Bart, and God had to break my big toe to stop me. Betty burst out in hysterical laughter.

Finally, she quit laughing. "If that's what it took, I'm with God."

I proceeded to tell her about Crystal's letter and how I refused to open it.

"Crystal is mad at you for two reasons. Firstly, because you *stopped Bart's abuse.* Secondly, because you *didn't stop it* until that morning you found his white satchel. You are in a *No Win Situation* with your daughter."

"What am I supposed to do now?"

"It is time for you to allow yourself to feel your emotions and properly grieve over this bad situation. I want you to write about your pain, go ahead and feel vulnerable, and cry or grieve about Crystal or what Bart did, whenever you feel it."

✳ ✳ ✳

Stacy dropped by a few days later to check on my injury and update me about his new position with Joseph G.

✳ ✳ ✳

When I returned to work for Joseph, he approached me. "Stacy, I'm proud of you. You're so young to have accomplished all of this. You had to learn to *plan your work and work your plan.*"

"Joseph, I need to thank you. I finally learned how to follow-through and do my job all by myself."

A smile crossed my face, when I heard Joseph say, "I'm proud of you, too, honey."

About a week later, I asked Joseph to be my Sponsor.

"Oh, Stacy, pick someone who has what you want and ask them, instead."

"I did. You're sober, drive a Mercedes, own a Penthouse and you have a business. That's what I want. I also want you for my AA Sponsor."

"I'd rather not be your Sponsor, since I'm your boss. I can't wear two hats at once in your life and be effective. I will help you with AA, until you find someone else."

What I didn't realize was the real reason Joseph declined. He was extremely attracted to me. Several weeks later, he invited me and Roy, someone he did sponsor in AA, to attend the Atlanta AA Roundup. Roy was a short, blond, macho-looking guy. Joseph paid my way to Atlanta, so I didn't worry about money. We still hadn't discussed my salary, and I had yet to receive my first paycheck. During our first night in Atlanta, we danced at *Rich's*, one of the gay bars on his sleeping giant prospectus list of purchases.

After we finished dancing, he drove us to an all-night place called *House of Pies*. We talked until dawn. During our conversation, I asked him a question. "Your bar deal had a captive audience, and it still does. It sounds like a guaranteed money-maker to me."

He waved his left hand in the air. "*Let my sleeping giant slumber.* Just forget it."

As we drove back to his office the next day, I rode in the front seat to quiz him again about the bar deal. Roy was asleep in the backseat, probably from boredom. By the time we saw our hometown skyline, I patted Joseph on his shoulder. "Let's wake up your Sleeping Giant in Atlanta!"

✳ ✳ ✳

On July 30, 1989, I received a phone call at work. It was Steve. "Crystal's in labor. We're at Freeman Hospital."

"I'll be there as soon as I can get permission from Ivan to leave work." I hung up, found Ivan, told him why I needed to leave for an hour or so. He made another hateful reply.

"Just how many kids is your daughter going to have, anyway?"

"Are you serious?"

"Oh, go on, but don't stay gone long." I turned to leave. *What is it with this awful man? I know he has a daughter.*

It was winter, and I wore my long, beige coat with a fluffy fur collar, as I entered the hospital carrying my purse and camera. I stopped at the Nurse's Desk. "I'm here to see my daughter, Crystal Simmons. She's about to have a baby."

A redheaded nurse said, "You will find her in Room 143."

I stopped in the hospital florist shop, bought a bouquet of flowers and a card, then I hurried down the hall to Crystal's room. Steve wasn't there, so I eased toward Crystal. "Hi, honey. How are you doing?"

She smiled. "Okay. Have you seen our little girl yet?"

"We got a girl this time?"

"Yes, we did. We named her Kay Marie."

The door opened and another nurse brought in Kay Marie and handed her to Crystal. I put her card and flowers on a table and leaned close to see her. "My goodness, she looks just like you, Crystal."

"Can I hold her for a few minutes? I have to get back to work before long."

Crystal let me hold her for a few minutes. Steve soon returned with flowers for her. "Steve, would you take my picture holding Kay Marie?"

"Of course I will!" He took our picture. I returned Kay Marie to Crystal, kissed Crystal on her cheek and returned to work. I had hopes that Crystal would finally be at peace."

✳ ✳ ✳

It was during this time that I was dancing more and more at the local *Parents Without Partners* group. One of the ladies named Diana Holder handed me a flyer one night. "Debbie, I hope you will join us on this fun trip to the Bahamas on September first."

I glanced at the flyer. "Wow, one week at a beautiful resort. I'm interested."

"Let me know by August tenth. That's when I will make our reservations. I'll also need your payment by then."

"Sounds like great fun! Count me in."

✳ ✳ ✳

Stacy dropped by the house unexpectedly the following Saturday. I could sense that he wanted to talk, so I handed him a soda pop, got one for me, and we sat on the den couch.

"How are things in your world these days?"

"Since I'm in AA, I want to be honest with you. This is about Bill H. You thought I was working for Bill. I wasn't. The truth is, I was being kept by him, and Dolan wasn't his son. He was like me regarding Bill. Our common interest was Bill's money. The thing that surprised Bill was that I had a genuine interest in learning the ropes of his movie business. Dolan didn't. I have *no regrets* about any part of what I did. Jetting around the country in his plane was great fun."

"Thank you for being honest with me about Bill. I had always wondered about his strong interest in you."

Stacy paused. "Now that I'm working for Joseph, he's been taking me out to dinner and courting me. His attachment started when we danced in Atlanta recently. I think he wants it so much, because I'm the first person in his life who is truly interested in *how* he does business. My main concern is to avoid another Bill situation with a bad ending. Yesterday, Joseph made me an offer. 'Well, I've been thinking about your salary since our trip, and this is what I've thought about doing. I will pay you fifteen-hundred-dollars a month salary, but I want to make you another offer. If you'll come to my Penthouse once a month and give me a blow job, I'll pay you twenty-five-hundred-dollars a month.' "

"I turned my head, tried not to act shocked, and replied, 'No thanks. I'll take the fifteen-hundred.'"

"Mom, he's going to pay me fifteen-hundred-dollars-a-month, after I led him on so well. Oddly, I did it just as well as he could have. Joseph is one slick salesman when it comes to business."

"What are you trying to tell me about him?"

"He wants me to move in with him. He bought tickets and made plans for two in San Francisco next weekend."

"Are you going to accept his offer?"

"I've been stalling him. I just don't know yet."

"That's a big decision, especially due to your age difference."

"Joseph's new business is going great. He showed me plans to move his office to a high-rise complex across town, complete with five salesmen and six vice president assistants."

"He recently bragged to me. 'Stacy, this is the perfect *boiler room* setup. Robert Redford, eat your heart out!' "

✳ ✳ ✳

When I saw Betty T. the following week, I ran Stacy's potential plans by her.

"How does that make you feel to know that Stacy may move in with another older man?"

"It isn't what I would choose for him. He must live with his choices and the results."

"What about Joseph's apparent dishonesty in business?"

"I don't like it, but what can I do?"

"You can confront Stacy about it, before it gets him in trouble when Joseph gets in trouble."

"You're right. I wouldn't like that at all."

"If you saw Stacy playing in the street as a child, would you tell him that the street isn't a safe place to play?"

"Of course, I would."

"This is no different. It sounds as if Joseph is a shady businessman. I know you don't want Stacy in trouble with the Law."

"No, I certainly don't."

"Now, let's discuss your past again. I find that it is the *person you defend* that I look to as the real offender in your life. Your mother is the offender from the *victim position,* and that is so hard to work with, because she wasn't open or blatant about it. These types are sneaky and want to look good to others. If you look to her about it, it makes you feel crazy, since she is so *innocent looking.*"

Betty's observation stunned me. *I would have never thought of Mother as the main offender in my life.*

"I want you to admit to yourself that she was cruel, mean and selfish to you, and that you are totally okay. Debbie, if you had heard your story, and it was about me instead of you, you would think it was horrible. Right?"

I slowly nodded in agreement.

"I have noted how you go into pain and tears when you discuss things she did to you over the years, and then, you begin to laugh and smile about it. It is as if you continue to give your mother a pass for her offenses."

"Betty, I made my amends to Mother, because I told her that I hated her during my Senior Year in high school."

"You had a *right to hate her*. Look at all of the abusive things she did and said to you during that difficult time in your life."

Betty's assessment made me cry.

"Your mother left you, and also your older brother, alone at night when you were both so young. She didn't nurture either one of you. She shifted her decision onto you about who should leave; you or Harry. She pushed you into a marriage to save her own face. She stripped you of your dignity, friends and graduation ceremony. Then, she threw you out of her house, knowing you had nowhere to go and no money. She also took back your car and bedroom furniture, and later gave the bedroom suite to Crystal."

I kept my head bowed in sorrow for my past life and what I had endured from Mother while growing up.

"Your mother is very good at taking care of herself, and maybe, she should *not have ever had any children*. This next week, I want you to remember that you are a wonderful, caring and honest person who didn't deserve to be treated as you were."

✳ ✳ ✳

A month passed when Steve phoned. "Crystal has left me again."

"This can't be happening. Where did she go?"

"I don't know. I spoke with her gynecologist. He told me that it could be that when her milk comes in, she gets Postpartum Depression, and the more children she has, the more likely she is to be depressed in each subsequent pregnancy."

"I haven't noticed her being depressed. Have you?"

"I'm not sure."

"Now that she has four children, maybe she shouldn't have any more kids."

"I'm going to have to find someone to babysit the kids, since I have to work. Hopefully, she will come to her senses and show up real soon."

"I'll let you know if I hear from her."

✷ ✷ ✷

A month passed and no Crystal. I was reclined on my couch nursing a migraine headache, when my phone rang.

"Great news, Crystal came home and agreed to see her doctor. He put her on Paxil to treat her depression."

"Let's hope it keeps her on an even keel. Keep me posted if things go downhill again."

✷ ✷ ✷

The time for my Bahama vacation was finally only two weeks away. I asked Stacy to come by once to check on my mail and the house while I was gone. I remember getting my big suitcase from the garage and taking it to my bedroom. Suddenly, an old familiar pain hit my right side. I doubled up in extreme pain and reclined on my bed for fifteen minutes. Finally, I sat up and realized it was the same pain I had right after my second surgery. All I could think was, *"Please, God, not a third surgery in such a short time!'*

I phoned my brother, Matt. When he answered his phone, I broke into tears. "I don't know what to do. The pain in my side just returned. I've already had two surgeries. This should not be happening to me again."

"Sis, I want you to look in the Yellow Pages, find a good Oncologist and make an emergency appointment for today. Then, you drive to Dr. K's office unannounced and demand all of your records be released to you while you wait."

"Can I do that?"

"You sure can. Don't let that doctor tell you otherwise."

I hung up, found an Oncologist named Dr. B. in the Yellow Pages, made an emergency appointment, and then, I drove to Dr. K.'s office and walked inside. I did exactly as Matt had directed. "I want every record and x-ray in my file released to me immediately. I will wait."

The nurse got huffy with me. "Not without notice."

"Consider this my notice. I won't leave until you comply."

She jumped up and went to speak to Dr. K. Finally, she returned with everything I had requested in a large manila envelope. I took the envelope and drove to Dr. B's office.

✳ ✳ ✳

When I entered Dr. B's office, I handed his nurse the large envelope. Five minutes later, she escorted me to his office to speak with him. Dr. B. had reddish hair, and a warm smile. He rose and shook my hand. When he sat down at his desk, I sat across from him. I related the horror of my past two surgeries since January 16, 1989. "Can you help me get this pain stopped?"

"First, I want to do an examination, and then, I will know more about what is going on and what I can do about it."

He called his nurse on his phone. She quickly escorted me into an Exam Room. After I put on a paper gown, his nurse had to help me onto the exam table. Dr. B. made his exam and left the room. His nurse helped me off the exam table. "Please dress. Dr. B. wants to talk to you in his office."

I did as requested, and she led me back into Dr. B.'s office. I eased into the chair across from him. "So, can you stop this horrible pain?"

His warm smile calmed me down. "I'm *so* glad you're here. Otherwise, *you would be dead in one year from ovarian cancer.* That sliver of ovary embedded in the lining of your stomach has to come out. It is diseased, and before long, it will shoot you full of cancer like a shotgun blast. From what I can see in your records and my exam, I can safely remove it and have you back on your feet in four weeks."

I tried not to cry. "I've already paid for a one week vacation with friends to the Bahamas. I want to go on my trip first."

Dr. B. shook his head. "What will happen if you get there and the pain grows worse, and they have to put you in a hospital? I won't be there to take care of you."

"I'm willing to take that chance. I have my heart set on going on this trip."

Dr. B. stood up and shook my hand. "See you on September eighth for surgery." He grinned. "*Don't be late!*"

10

≈

It's Tough, But It's Love

When I woke up after my third surgery, Dr. B. was standing there with a big grin. He took my hand. "Everything went fine. Don't expect any more pain. I completely removed that sliver of ovary. You will be able to return to work in four weeks."

"Thank you for saving my life!"

Dr. B. blushed and left my room. Later, Stacy came by and brought me flowers. Crystal never called or came to see me.

One of my longtime friends named Dee did call me. "I just heard about your surgery. How did it go?"

"This is my third surgery in nine months caused by two doctors who could have killed me. Thankfully, my brother convinced me to find an Oncologist who could help me."

"Debbie, I've always heard it said, *'Doctors bury their mistakes!'* Thank the Lord, you found a good doctor!"

When Stacy drove me home from the hospital, he handed me a stack of mail from my mailbox. Then, he went to buy me some diet pop at the store. While he was gone, I opened my mail. The last letter was from Bart, but the address looked odd. I opened his envelope and read the contents.

"Hi goodlookin', *I'm back at Club Fed enjoying more free room-and-board again. Shucks, I just can't seem to stay out of trouble. Had a little problem with my employer, got mad and did some*

stuff I guess I shouldn't have done. Write me when you have time. Love you beautiful woman! ***Bart.****"*

Stacy soon returned from the store. "Well, Bart's back in prison again. I swear he must like being locked up."

"Mom, forget him. He's nothing but bad news." *I glanced at my still healing big toe.*

"You're right, honey. How is your job with Joseph going?"

"We moved into a new office building. When you can drive again, I want you to drop by for a visit."

"Okay, I will in a couple of weeks."

"I wrote Pia Mellody a letter last week. I asked her if there is a connection between being sexually abused and love addiction."

"I bet she will send you a reply."

"We'll see."

✳ ✳ ✳

A week before Dr. B. would allow me to return to work, I went to see my psychic that I had been visiting for many years named Bonnae M. She was a heavyset, sweet lady and extremely accurate in her readings. When I knocked on her door, she opened her door. Her office was filled with pictures and statues of various Angels. It always made me feel so peaceful and at home. She sat down and handed me a small card. "Jot down your name, birthday and three favorite colors on this card." While I wrote my info, she shuffled her deck of cards many times. After I handed her the info card, she instructed, "Now shuffle the cards and cut them three times."

Bonnae looked at each card on the top of my stack of three card cuts and gave me some important information about each card. Next, she placed each top card on the table and added a total of ten cards to each card in a rotating fashion.

During the reading, she predicted the following things.

"The love of a child is good and negative from Crystal. Trouble with your daughter is coming. Unpleasant doors are opening with her."

"There's an upcoming argument with your mother."

"Crystal has given up her freedom in her church."

"Who is George? You will meet him in the near future."

"If Stacy's temperament turns negative, you may need to dial 911. He is a boy-like-man. He may be incarcerated. He has financial trouble. Don't let him come home right now. He will sap your energy if you aren't careful."

"I see *many changes* coming with your son. There's a big argument with your daughter on the way."

"Your ex will hurt you if you see him. Don't do it."

"Which ex-husband are you talking about, Bonnae?"

"The one who is getting a divorce."

"I don't know which one that would be."

"Doors are opening. Make no mistakes. Your boy will go with you. He will move to a coastal town in the near future. He is not so gay, since he has a fear of AIDS."

"Who is Lori? She's been sick."

"Yes, she has. She had a miscarriage recently."

"There is trouble with a child coming from your daughter."

"Wow! It sounds like I have a load of trouble coming down the pike."

Bonnae counted my Angels in the cards she had spread out at the beginning of my reading. "You have thirteen Angels; one High Arch Angel, eight Guardian Angels and four small Angels. They will watch over you through the coming difficulty."

She held my hands and said a prayer for me. After I paid her, she gave me a hug. I left with my notebook. I always took notes when I saw Bonnae, in order to track her accuracy. Over the years, she has been 85 percent accurate. Plus, she always told me; *"Psychics don't do time well."* I have found that to be a true statement.

✻ ✻ ✻

It was October 3, 1990, I was due to return to work the next day. I decided to go see Stacy's new office building, when my phone message light came on. I listened to it. "Debbie, this is Jack." *Instant rage shot through me like a tidal wave to hear that hideous monotone voice again.* "You wouldn't see me the last time I was in town to meet Crystal. I'm getting a divorce. I'm a changed man now, and I'd like to see you again." *The audacity of this despicable man, after all he did to me. As if I'd give the SOB a ninth chance to kill me. And to think, he walked out of Crystal's life just a mere 27 years ago. Bonnae was correct on this prediction right away.*

✻ ✻ ✻

I drove across town to see Stacy's new office building. When I walked in, he was on the phone arguing with someone. He motioned for me to sit down, as he continued with his conversation. "Don't you dare do that to us!" He slammed his phone down.

"Sounds like a bad disagreement."

"It's our Building Manager. She's threatening to have us evicted."

"Why?"

"We haven't paid our lease fee in months."

"Honey, that's not the way to do business."

"So what?"

"I see you on a different path that can lead to bad problems, and that worries me. Can I share my concern with you?"

"Yeah."

"I'm afraid Joseph's business tactics will land both of you in big trouble with the Law, and I don't want to see that happen."

"Oh, so you're calling us *evil*."

"No, I'm not saying that. I see bad choices being made that can lead to serious problems, and that worries me."

"I'm not ready to be scrutinized for who or what I am. I respect Joseph as a businessman. All of your *Betty Talk* gets on my nerves."

"So, I can't scrutinize you, but you just scrutinized me. And now, you tell me how much you respect someone you have labeled as a *true con-artist.* That kind of logic bothers me. Betty *did not force* me to talk to you about this. I chose to do it myself, because I love you."

"Mother, if you loved me, you would have taken the time to lovingly suggest I reconsider certain choices I made."

"That's what I just did, honey."

"You have never been a good Mother!"

"I will not be dishonest to make you feel better. No deeply rooted habit of self-justification can explain away our faults."

"Why don't you just leave? I never want to see you again!"

"If that's what you want. Let me remind you that I made my amends to you about the things I wish I could have done better as you were growing up. I don't pretend to be perfect, but my *perfectly imperfect imperfections* allows me to continue to grow in love and truth."

"Get out of my life. Go grow in *love and truth* somewhere else."

"Never forget, I love you and care about you and your future. I hope you will learn to only say words which are music to your ears and to those of others."

✳ ✳ ✳

Two weeks later, I called Crystal. "Hi honey, I'd like to keep Daniel for the weekend. I sure do miss him."

"Okay, if you will meet me halfway to your house. I don't want to drive all the way there."

"How about nine a.m. Saturday morning at McDonald's?"

✳ ✳ ✳

On Saturday, I arrived at McDonald's on time. Crystal was twenty minutes late. Daniel hurried out of her car and hopped into my car. "Hi, sweetheart. I've missed you!"

"I missed you, too, Nana!"

"What would you like to do for fun today?"

"I want to see the new *Robin Hood* movie."

"Sounds good to me. We'll get a bite to eat and then go to the Red Rock Mall to see the movie.

"I love you, Nana!"

"You know how much I love you!" I squeezed his arm. "Sometimes, I wish you were still living with me."

"Me, too!"

Daniel and I enjoyed *Robin Hood* a lot. Afterward, he tugged on my arm. "Nana, can we stop by the video game place?"

"Sure, there's one in the Red Rock Mall." He was a whiz on video games. Then, I tapped his arm. "Time to go. I'm almost out of money."

"I thought you were rich, Nana."

His comment made me laugh. "I wish!"

I stopped for gas. Daniel went inside while I paid for it. Some comic books caught his eye. "Nana, can I have just one?"

"Sure you can."

He picked out *Daredevil #1*. I paid the clerk, filled up my gas tank and drove us home.

✳ ✳ ✳

The next morning, Daniel wanted to swim in my pool, so I joined him. We climbed the ladder and slid into the pool over and over. Too quickly, four p.m. arrived. "Daniel, time to get you changed. I need to get you back to your Mom."

"Aw, do I have to go so soon?"

"Afraid so."

We went inside and dressed. Then, I phoned Crystal. "Hi honey, I'm heading to McDonald's to drop Daniel off with you."

"I'll be there at six p.m."

When Daniel and I arrived, there was no Crystal. We waited and waited. Finally, Steve showed up. I walked Daniel to his car. "Is everything okay, Steve? I was expecting to see Crystal."

"Oh, it's nothing. Just a little disagreement."

I kissed Daniel, and he got into Steve's car. Daniel waved as they drove out of sight. I was back home in thirty minutes. When I walked in, my phone was ringing.

"What were you thinking by taking Daniel to see *Robin Hood* and buying him that *Daredevil* comic book?"

"What does that mean? The movie was rated PG, and the comic book is from Marvel."

"Don't you ever take him to another movie, until I give you the okay. The same goes for comic books."

"Crystal, there was nothing about the movie that would bother Daniel, and I liked *Daredevil* comics when I was a kid."

"My church believes that *Robin Hood* is a fairytale, *and they are of the Devil.* I believe that *Daredevil* is unacceptable for my son to read."

"You've got to be kidding!"

"No, I'm dead serious."

"You and that church of yours..." She hung up on me.

My head was reeling. *Is there a full moon tonight?*

✳ ✳ ✳

Since both of my kids weren't speaking to me, I decided to join a Singles Group at a Methodist Church across town. I found the group friendly, and discovered that Methodists actually allow dancing. *That works for me, because I'm weary of those cult churches.*

One guy in the group, J.D., asked for my phone number. I gave it to him. He called me a week later for a date to go C&W dancing. He was a good dancer, and I enjoyed his company. Yet, there was something about him that gave me the impression he might be gay. Rather than a date, I agreed to meet him at a C&W dance spot. Not once did he ever try to kiss me, even for a peck on the cheek. I never knew for sure, but my gut feeling was steady, he could be gay.

When the group arranged a ski trip to Colorado for November first, I decided to join them and had a blast.

As Thanksgiving approached, I returned to PWP for their Thanksgiving Dance. I wandered around the room to find a seat, when someone tapped my shoulder. I turned and there stood Jay. "Hey, baby, longtime no see."

"That's true." I saw an empty spot at a table and sat down. He pulled up a chair from another table and joined me.

"I've missed my baby." He put his beer bottle on the table.

"Jay, if only you didn't drink so much, but you do." I looked at his bloodshot eyes.

"I'll quit drinking, if that's what it takes to get you back."

"I don't want to go thru that again. You aren't the same person when you're drunk."

"I won't get drunk anymore, Scout's Honor."

"You weren't a Boy Scout, were you?"

He gave me his shit-eatin' grin. "No."

About that time, a guy I didn't know tapped me on my shoulder. "Would you like to dance?"

"Sure." I got up and danced two dances with him.

When I sat back down, Jay was still there. "You could at least dance a few dances with me."

"Just two dances, but no more." He held me ultra-close and squeezed my right hand like a vice. "Please don't squeeze my hand. That hurts."

"I want you back. I won't take 'No' for an answer."

"Absolutely not!" He squeezed my hand even harder. I yanked my hand loose and walked off the floor.

He yelled, "Bitch!"

One of my dance friends named Curt, came over and sat beside me. He was a truck driver, so I felt protected. Suddenly, Jay stormed to our table. "You're in my seat, buddy, and she's my girl, so get lost!"

Curt stood up. "I'll tell you once. Leave her alone."

Jay cussed all the way to the front door and left.

"Thanks, Curt."

"When you're ready to leave, I'll walk you to your car just in case that jerk is waiting out there."

At closing time, Curt walked me to my car. "Go ahead and drive home. If I see him follow you off the lot, I'll be right behind him."

"Thanks again, Curt!"

I made it home just fine and fell asleep quickly.

✳ ✳ ✳

The next morning, I opened my front door to get my newspaper. I was startled to see that a pair of wet lips had kissed the glass on my storm door. Drool ran all the way down the window. Chills went all over me, followed by anger. I went to my phone and phoned Jay. "I know you did that to my door and it better not happen again!"

"I don't know what you're talking about."

"Oh yes you do. Just stay away from me!"

That night I had a strange dream. I saw girls of stair-step ages. I cried, as I spoke to each of them and said, "Goodbye." Then, it hit me, each girl was me at a different age, when I was growing up.

✳ ✳ ✳

A few days later my phone rang and I answered. "Hello Mother."

"Crystal, Daniel and the kids just left here."

"How was your visit? Crystal's not speaking to me."

"That's what I heard. Daniel was just *awful* the whole afternoon."

"What did he do?"

"He told me that you took him to see a *naughty movie.*"

"It wasn't naughty. It was *Robin Hood.* Crystal informed me that her church believes *fairytales are of the Devil, and comic books are evil.* What next?"

"Debbie, I want you to take Daniel away from Crystal, before she completely ruins him."

"I can't do that. Kids need their mother."

"Yes, you can, and I'll pay for it."

"No, I raised my children. Crystal needs to raise her kids."

"I can't let her fill their heads full of *Devil Worship drivel!*"

"Maybe, in time, she'll come to her senses."

"If I wasn't so old, I'd take Daniel away from her myself."

✳ ✳ ✳

During my next visit with Betty, I told her what had recently transpired with my family and also about my unusual dream.

"How did those events with both children make you feel?"

"They made me angry and sick at my stomach."

"Those are *carried feelings.* I want to talk about the two nightmares you've been having since childhood about an elephant or a big gorilla chasing you? Are you still having them?"

"Off-and-on, yes, I am."

"I want you to see yourself as eight and sitting in a chair in front of you. Now, tell me how you felt at that age."

"I was sad, lonely, afraid and intimidated."

"What can you do for her?"

"Try to make her feel better."

"How will you do that?"

"I'm not sure."

"Your mother and Crystal are *selfish, immature and are not in recovery. They have a lot in common.* I want you to find out your mother's wedding date to your dad. During your next visit, we will talk about it. I also want you to call Crystal since you are doing so well and that will affirm it."

✱ ✱ ✱

I phoned Mother the next morning. "Mother, what was the date of your marriage to my dad?"

"I can't remember."

"You can't? Oh, come on. Surely you do."

There was a lengthy pause. "It was June 9, 1942." Then, she changed the subject. "You know, I gave you some insurance money about eight years ago."

"Yes, but I hadn't asked for it. Why did you do that?"

"I don't recall."

All I could do was shake my head. "Call you next week."

I hung up, took a deep breath and called Crystal. "Hi honey, how about we have lunch together on Saturday as my treat?"

"Okay, where and what time."

"Make it noon at Joseph's Seafood Grill on Main Street."

Crystal was waiting in the lobby when I arrived. A hostess seated us in a booth. "I want us to work things out. We're family, and you are very important to me."

"Okay, but I set the rules for Daniel, not you." I nodded.

"Crystal, I'd really like for you to consider having a visit with my psychotherapist, Betty T. She's helped me a lot so far, and I believe you will benefit by talking with her." I handed her one of Betty T.'s business cards.

✳ ✳ ✳

On Sunday, I received a call from a gay friend of Stacy's named, Danny S. "Debbie, you need to know something about Stacy."

"What would that be?"

"Stacy just found out that Joseph G. has AIDS."

My heart stopped. "Oh no! What about Stacy?"

"He assured me that he doesn't have it."

Tears rolled down my cheeks. "Thank God!"

"I know Stacy misses you. Why don't you call him? Please don't tell him what I just said. I don't want him mad at me."

"I promise, not a word about your call."

✳ ✳ ✳

I hung up and phoned Stacy. "Hi honey, I sure do miss you."

"Mom, I'm glad you called. Joseph is sick with AIDS. I was tested yesterday, and I'm okay."

"Thank goodness!"

"Joseph's birthday is close. His family is going to throw him a party. They asked me to invite you."

"I would like that very much."

"When they pick a day and time, I'll let you know."

I hung up. *How can one person live through my life and remain sane? Only by the Grace of God.*

Three weeks passed, when Stacy dropped by the house one day. "Mom, I finally got a reply from Pia to my letter. I thought you might like to read it."

"Of course, I would." He handed me Pia's reply.

"Dear Stacy, I believe sex addiction is primarily caused by childhood sexual abuse. I don't know if it (sexual abuse) has to do with sexual preference, but I do know it impacts addicted compulsive sexual experience. So, I never tell anyone who is gay that the abuse they have had has set up their homosexuality. Nobody really knows. I support and admire your recovery. Warm regards, Pia."

I returned the letter to Stacy. *"Is that the reply that you expected?"*

11

≈

When the Student Is Ready

"Her reply encourages me to continue with my AA meetings, read recovery books by Pia and Bob S. and listen to recovery tapes by Bob E. I want my AA recovery to move forward. Without that, I would fall off of the wagon again."

"I'm so glad to hear your dedication to your recovery. I've been wondering how Joseph revealed to you that he had AIDS."

"It happened the day I brought home some Christmas decorations in preparation for buying our Christmas tree. He was resting on our couch."

"Stacy, come sit beside me. I have something to tell you."

"I had no idea what he was about to tell me."

"This is my last Christmas. Time is short."

"I couldn't believe my ears. 'You're only fifty-two. I've never seen you give up on anything before.'"

"His weight loss had tipped me off that he might be living with full-blown AIDS and wouldn't see another year through."

"I'm sorry. I know how much Joseph has meant to you."

"By the way, Mom, his birthday party is set for this Saturday night. I can pick you up at six p.m."

***

Stacy arrived promptly and drove us to Joseph's birthday party. It was held at his brother's home in an affluent part of town.

When the door opened, Joseph greeted us wearing a colorful birthday hat. "Debbie, I'm so glad you came. By the way, my ex-wife, Nancy, is here along with most of my family."

Everything that evening was happy, light-spirited and enjoyable. Joseph even played the piano briefly for us, and we sang *Happy Birthday* to him. I could see that he had lost a lot of weight. He stood up, took a bow, put his arm around his mother's shoulders and made a speech that made us laugh, instead of cry.

I waited until we were on our way home to ask Stacy a question. "I thought Joseph's ex-wife was mad at him."

"She was, but he always manages to handle every serious moment with humor. He had maneuvered funds for his money management company idea by convincing her to sell one of the expensive furs and some of her diamond jewelry he'd given her during their 12 year marriage. When she learned about his serious health condition, she was one of the first to call him."

✳ ✳ ✳

My phone rang the next day. I hesitated for fear that Joseph had died.

"Mom, Steve and I are leaving for California in three weeks with the kids."

"Are you driving or flying?"

"We're driving there to visit with my dad."

"Okay. I hope he doesn't disappoint you."

"He won't. He's a changed man, and he quit drinking."

"I hope you're right. Have a good trip."

✳ ✳ ✳

It was time for another visit with Betty. As I sat down, she sipped her hot tea. "Tell me all about your last two weeks."

"Work related or otherwise?"

She laughed. "No, no, you don't. I want to know how your weeks were for *you*."

I brought her up-to-date on the family events since our last visit, and how Mother claimed she couldn't recall her marriage date to my dad.

"How did you feel when your mother claimed she couldn't recall her marriage date?"

"I was surprised."

"It's called *denying your reality*. Your mother denied a lot of your reality over the years. You parented your mother, step-father and three husbands. Even your world at work expects it. Your brother parented you a little, and he probably resented it, since no one ever parented him."

"I never looked at things that way."

"That is enough to make anyone tired, lonely and quite depressed."

"Yeah, Mother even asked me to call Pop Sherman's son last year, after he almost caught his home on fire. She wanted me to convince him to put Pop Sherman into a Nursing Home. He refused to help and told Pop Sherman about my call. Now, he's mad at me."

"It was your Mother's job, *not yours*. Once more, you did more parenting of her."

"I understand what you're saying. How do I stop it?"

"By *allowing others to own their own reality*, instead of you doing it. Stop getting sucked in as everyone's rescuer. In two weeks, we'll work on your father and step-father issues. Write down three adjectives to describe each of them and six reasons why you are still angry at them."

"By the way, when I had lunch with Crystal, I also asked her to consider having a visit with you sometime."

"What was her response?"

"There wasn't one that I could see, but I gave her one of your business cards."

Betty nodded with a grin.

✳ ✳ ✳

At work on Monday, Lori approached me about a remark that several co-workers made about me. "After you declined to be their representative anymore, most of the guys called you a *company lover.*"

Normally, I would have taken the bait and caused a scene. That time I didn't. "It's their opinion. What do you want me to do about it?"

"Well, I thought you'd go say something to them."

"No, I'm not going to do that. You can if you want to though."

Her face fell. "Oh, I can't believe you're going to let them get away with it."

"Feel free to defend me, if you want."

I turned, walked to my work area, and left Lori to deal with her own thoughts and reality. *I'm tired of being everyone's rescuer.* I smirked to myself. *Betty would be proud of me.*

✳ ✳ ✳

The next day at work, Lori came and found me. "Debbie, you have a phone call on the lunchroom phone."

"Any idea who it is?"

"I think it might be Crystal."

I scurried to the lunchroom phone and said, "Crystal?"

"Mom, I've made a decision."

"Okay, let's hear it."

"Will you keep Kay Marie, while I have my first visit with Betty tomorrow morning?"

At first, I was speechless, and then I teared up. "You know I will, honey. This is such great news!"

The next day couldn't arrive soon enough. I entertained Kay Marie, while Crystal talked with Betty. After her hour ended, Crystal came out of the session and had obviously been crying.

"Mom, I like Betty."

Betty opened her door and waived. "See you in two weeks, Crystal. Have a good trip to California to see your dad."

We rode the elevator down to the parking garage and entered Crystal's SUV. As she drove me home, she surprised me. "Mom, I never realized it before, but I've never been allowed to make my own decisions. Not as a child with Bart, or when I married Oscar. My friends pushed me into that marriage. And with my marriage to Steve, I really had a choice, but I didn't realize I did. We should have just dated for one year. We're much better friends. I don't have *that feeling* with him like I do with *you know who!*"

"Eric?"

"Uh-huh!"

"I understand. That's how I always felt about my high school sweetheart, too."

After Crystal dropped me off at home, I'm certain my feet never touched the ground as I walked into my home.

✳ ✳ ✳

Joseph died three weeks later. I wasn't at the hospital, but Stacy came by the following week to talk about it.

"Mom, I was wrong in my prediction about Joseph. I never thought I could fall for him. This time, I honestly fell in love with the older man who had the money and power. Unlike Bill, I truly loved Joseph *for better or worse, in sickness and in health, 'til death do us part.*"

"I discovered that Acquired Immune Deficiency Syndrome is a baffling disease. It proved more cunning than alcoholism, even though alcoholism kills countless millions every year. AIDS currently has no known cure. His health had become obvious to all his friends."

"We spent our last days together, like Laura and Dr. Zhivago did in their deserted winter palace, waiting and knowing that the Communists would come for us eventually. AIDS marched in like the Red Army. One evening, he was fine. The next, he was in the Freeman Emergency Room."

"That was on a Monday. By Wednesday, they told me he could go home by Thursday. On Thursday, they said that he wouldn't live through the night and placed him on oxygen."

"I watched him valiantly struggle, but his breathing tightened. It was painful to admit to myself that the end was near. It was devastating to watch him die from a simple strain of pneumonia virus that any healthy human being's immune system could have killed off over ten times a day."

"Our immune system is the life raft which protects us from harmful bacteria and viruses. When Joseph's life raft began to sink, all he could cling to was his warm, wonderful humor. The end drew closer and closer. I shared his last night with his family and ex-wife, Nancy. We stood around his hospital bedside and approached him."

"Do you need anything, Joseph?'"

"Yeah, I need some money! Nancy, get my passport. I'm crossing over!"

"Our tears switched to laughter. That's how he wanted it. His eyes closed, as his spirit departed this life. There still remained a smile on his lips, as if he laughed all the way into the Great Beyond."

People Viewing the AIDS Memorial Quilt in DC

✳ ✳ ✳

"Dr. Alec R., minister of one of the State's largest Methodist Churches, who was later accused of sexual abuse by multiple church workers, held the service for Joseph at the Red Rock Chapel. I was talking to several AA friends, when I saw you approaching before the funeral, Mom. Instantly, you gave me one of your warm hugs."

"Stacy, I'm so sorry about Joseph."

"A lot of people are, Mom. Thanks for coming."

"I was glad to see you, but I didn't have the heart to tell you then that Greg W. didn't make it So, I told you weeks later. He committed suicide on Christmas Day. His mother found him in his bed. He died from a drug overdose."

"How sad, and he was in AA and also my Al-Anon group."

"You saw how that little Red Rock Chapel overflowed with Joseph's family and multitude of friends, both gay and straight. The services seemed like a dream happening to someone else instead of Joseph. Then, *deja vue* hit me. My mind flashed through old scenes from Patty's funeral. Many times, I have wondered what happened in the Freeman Emergency Room that dark September morning when Patty was admitted as *Miss X.*"

"Through Joseph's death, I saw the *Gift of Life* and the *Mystery of Tragedy* that snatched an 18-year-old girl named Patty from my world. Alcoholism, AIDS and drugs are not the enemy. When Joseph's flame began to flicker out, I realized for the first time that *I had been the problem with my own life all along. We are our own enemy, and the enemy lives within.*"

12

≈

The Wind of Why

My phone rang after I came home from work the next night. It was a hysterical call from Crystal. "Mom, can you believe that my dad actually tried to spank my children, and I had to stop him? We're cutting our trip short and driving back home shortly."

"That doesn't surprise me at all. You needed to find out about your dad's horrible temper for yourself. I know that I told you how he tried to spank you when you were only six-months-old. You were teething, we argued, and he marched me upstairs into his Mom's room and threatened to kill me. He'll never change."

I could barely hear Crystal through her sobs. "I remember how he hurt you, but I wanted to believe he could change."

"It's okay, honey. I went back to him seven times. Thank God, you saw the real person before he hurt you or the kids."

❋ ❋ ❋

The following week, I was approached by several co-workers and Lori. "Our Local Union President isn't running for re-election. Don't want you to run for his office?"

"I don't think so. People don't appreciate it, when I stand up for them and put my neck on the line."

I walked away, and later, I received a phone call from the current Union President who was stepping down. "Debbie, you are the only person in this Local Union who can handle this position. I watched you in meetings and read the appeals you wrote to protect several worker's jobs. Please consider it."

"I'll think about it, but I have a lot going on in my life right now. I doubt it."

After I got home that night, I received another phone call. This one was from our International Union Rep, Kent F. "Nancy, we need you to consider running for office. You're co-workers need you. The Local and International Union both need you."

"It's a lot to consider. I don't know if I'm up to it. Let me sleep on it."

The next morning, I woke up and phoned the Local Union Secretary. "Put my name on the ballot for President."

When I hung up, I thought about what Betty had just taught me. "Stop getting sucked in as everyone's rescuer." *Here I go again, one more time. That's when I swear I heard the word 'Why' swish back-and-forth past my left ear several times.*

Two weeks later, I was elected President of my Local Union. Since I had been a union member for many years, I had to admit that it felt good to be given that honor.

✳ ✳ ✳

My home phone rapidly grew ultra-busy after my election. I kept a legal notepad by my phone to document every phone call.

Crystal phoned me. "Mom, I'm going to see Betty sooner."

"Because of the incident in California with your dad?'

"No, I mentioned to Steve what Betty said about control and decisions. He called her. She told him that I need to come back every week. She also told him, *'Crystal is in a crisis situation.'* "

"From what I can see, I totally agree with Betty." I could sense an explosive change on Crystal's horizon.

✳ ✳ ✳

Three days later, our Chapel Chairman, Nola K., phoned me. "Ivan just fired Sassy Hall. I approached the company about a meeting with Production Manager, Allen Cole. I want you to be with me in the meeting."

"Okay. When is it set for?"

"Friday at two p.m."

"Give me the details, so I can get prepared."

"Sassy was set up by Ivan's assistant, Ruby Hart, who claimed she intentionally screwed up an ad in her department."

"Get a signed statement from Sassy about Ruby and Ivan's conversations with her, so I can read them before the meeting."

I hung up my phone and it rang again. It was my brother, Matt. "Sis, I need to talk to you about something."

"Is it Mother?"

"No, it's about me."

"What's going on?"

"I've never once cheated on my wife of many years, but I have developed a strong friendship with a female that I golf with. It bothers me that we have an attraction. I want your opinion."

"From personal experience, I can say that this also happened to me at work. As long as you don't sleep with her, and you keep it on a friendship level, you aren't doing anything wrong. Strong attractions just happen sometimes."

"You don't think any less of me for this, do you?"

"Of course not, you're my brother, and I love you."

"I love you, too, Sis."

When I hung up the phone, I was so surprised that Matt thought enough of me to confide his problem to me. It made me feel good that we were getting closer, even though I seldom ever saw him due to the great distance between our locations.

✳ ✳ ✳

I was ready for some dancing, so I checked out the Methodist Singles Group's weekly schedule. They were going to meet at *Studebakers* on Thursday night to dance.

When I entered Studebakers, I joined several members of the Singles Group and took a seat. I remember wearing an orange dress with lace across the shoulders. I pulled my hair up in curls. Suddenly, George Austin approached and asked me to dance. I had met George several years ago at church. Lori dated him a few times, but she quickly stopped seeing him. George had big blue eyes and reminded me a lot of my dad, only shorter.

✻ ✻ ✻

Before I left for work the next day, I made many notes on my legal pad for the upcoming meeting on Sassy Hall's firing. While I was writing, Stacy knocked and then came in the house. "Hi Mom, I want to tell you my good news."

"What kind of good news, honey?"

"I rented an apartment near the Red Rock Tollway, and I got a job managing a gay bar."

"Great! What's your apartment address? I want to come see it sometime."

Stacy wrote his address on my legal pad. "I'd also like for you to drop by the club, after I get it set up my way."

"I can do that, too. What else is new?"

"I found Joseph's diary when I packed up things in our apartment."

"Find anything of interest that you didn't know?"

"Yes, he wrote, '*I'm in love with a wildcat.* He claims his life is not too exciting. I had to laugh. The young man has a sense of humor, especially after he talked about flying around the country in a private jet, meeting movie stars and living a luxurious life with Bill H., and he doesn't know it yet, but he's about to embark on another torrid affair with another rich, older man. Stacy is way too good-looking! I'm smitten.' "

"Stacy, keep those words tucked inside your heart for comfort."

✳ ✳ ✳

I phoned Lori Friday morning to discuss what she may have seen the night Ruby claimed Sassy had sabotaged an advertisement. Then, I listened intently to her description of the incident and took copious notes. "Thanks, Lori. I'll type this up so you can sign it."

I hung up, reread several pages in our Union Law Book, and then got ready for work. Two hours later, I arrived in the lunchroom thirty minutes early with a Company Contract, Union Law Book and legal pad filled with my notes inside a briefcase. I wore a shiny gray business suit and high heels.

Nola approached me. She was a nervous wreck, as she handed me Sassy's signed statement. I read it. Then, Nola leaned close and whispered. "What do you think? Can we save her job?"

"As far as I'm concerned, we can."

She threw her hands up. "Oh, I hope you're right."

Lori waved at me from the door of the ladies' room. I hurried inside, gave her the typed statement and she signed it.

Soon, Nola and I walked down the hall. I stepped into the Production Secretary's Office. "Tell Mr. Cole and Ivan that we'll be in the Conference Room for our meeting." She nodded.

We took our seats on the far side of the table. Mr. Cole and Ivan arrived five minutes later and closed the door.

I began. "Please tell me why you feel justified in firing Sassy Hall."

Ivan replied. "She destroyed company property, after she intentionally screwed up a large classified ad."

"How did she screw up the ad?"

"She put the wrong address and phone number on it which belonged to another company and cost us a lot of money."

"You are *certain* that she did this?"

Mr. Cole chimed in. "Ruby Hart would *never misrepresent the truth.*"

I opened my briefcase and pulled out Sassy's signed statement. "In this document, Sassy maintains that Ruby is the one who messed up the ad, so that she could get her fired."

Ivan snarled, "That isn't possible!"

"Are you sure?" I opened my notepad and read a statement from Lori. 'I, Lori Holland, saw Ruby Hart wait until Sassy went to the restroom. Then, she went to the page and changed the address and phone number line herself.' In essence, Sassy was set up by Ruby in order to get her fired."

Ivan stuttered. "She has to be lying."

Mr. Cole spoke up. "I need to talk to Ivan in my office." They stood up and left the Conference Room. Ten minutes later, Mr. Cole returned. "Sassy will be re-instated immediately."

"And nothing will appear in her personnel file about this?"

"That is correct."

Nola was speechless. We left the meeting. I went to find Sassy waiting in the lunchroom. "Sassy, your job is safe."

A look of shock covered her face. She slowly rose. "I know I haven't been very nice to you, Debbie. I can't believe you actually went to bat for me anyway." Then, she shook my hand.

"Sassy, I leave my personal feelings out of my role as President, because it's the professional way to hold office."

✷ ✷ ✷

After three peaceful weeks, Crystal and Steve showed up at my home. "To what do I owe the pleasure of your company today?"

Steve spoke first. "We want to ask you something."

"Okay, come inside."

They followed me into the den, and we all sat down. "Is this bad news?"

"In a way, yes. I wanted to be here when Crystal tells you what has happened."

"Let's hear it."

"Mom, Oscar is physically abusing Daniel."

I was stunned and angry. "You've got to be kidding."

"It's true. Daniel came home yesterday with bruises on his arms and face. When I asked about them, he said, 'Dad got mad at me and hit me. He also has refused to feed him if he gets hungry.'"

Because of my past childhood experience with my dad and Jack, I instantly doubled up my fists without realizing it.

"We are going to take him to a Red Rock Court and request Supervised Visitation for Daniel. Why we came here today is to ask if you will consider being our Supervised Visitation Agent for Daniel."

"What does that entail, Steve?"

"Oscar will only be able to see Daniel every-other-weekend and only in your presence for four hours. My attorney wants you to take notes about each visit for the judge."

"How long will this go on?"

"Until we have enough evidence to show the court that Oscar hasn't changed. Then, we will request that his visits stop while he takes mandatory counseling."

"I'm not going to let him hurt my grandson. Of course, I'll do it. When will it start, Crystal?"

"Next Saturday. It's only for four hours."

"How will Daniel get to my home?"

"One of us will bring him and pick him up after each visit."

"Okay, but I won't take any smart-mouth off of Oscar."

✳ ✳ ✳

I knew I had a visit with Betty the next day. I sat down at my kitchen table and jotted down three adjectives about my dad and step-dad, plus six reasons why I am still angry at them.

The next day in Betty's inner office, I updated her on my activities since I last saw her.

"And your list I asked you to make for me about your dad and step-dad?"

I handed her my sheet and watched as she read it. "What terrible parent figures. How do you feel about them and what you wrote?"

I couldn't respond.

"I want you to look at who each of your husbands was like."

All I could do was glance at Betty and then look away.

"Jack was like your dad. Tim was a carbon copy of your step-dad. Bart could have been your dad's brother. Can you see how your parents set you up to keep on failing?"

"Yes, but no."

"I want you to say how you would feel about this story, *if it had been Crystal's story instead of yours.*"

"I could do that. I'd be mad as hell!"

"So, why don't you feel that way for yourself?"

Again, I was totally speechless for a moment. "I don't know what to say."

"Let's sit and be quiet for a few minutes, or we can go on."

"Let's go on."

"It is time for you to begin grieving, instead of talking in a monotone voice. Let your feelings out. *Who you are is not your fault.* All three of your parents created the person you became."

I closed my eyes and continued to listen to Betty explain.

"*You are not to blame!* You had a clean slate when you were born. They wrote on it for you, and then, when you became who they set you up to be, *they disowned what they had created.* Your mother even thought of *dumping you into a girl's home.* It's no wonder you became full of despair and hopelessness and went into suicidal thoughts. When you went out of control as a teen, you were made to feel worthless for being that person."

I looked at Betty with tears in my eyes and got a Kleenex.

"Between now and our next visit, I want you to begin grieving for you and your childhood. You will feel empty at first, but in time, if you continue the grieving process, you will be able to fill that emptiness with totally new feelings. It will seem as if it is coming from a terrible place deep inside of a tall, dark forest that is scary and strange. You will feel lost and alone. But if you keep on going and don't turn back, a small light will appear. Eventually, you will reach the other side to a place you've never been before. *I promise you will receive a reward for your grieving.*"

It was impossible for me to respond, and even more impossible for me to stop the wave of tears that raced down my flushed cheeks.

"I don't know when, but the reward will come to you, Debbie. It is one of the promises of doing this grieving."

The next week, I spent lots of time thinking about everything Betty discussed during our last visit. I began to experience intermittent bouts of unexpected sadness and tears. My dreams were difficult. It was as if my mind wanted to review each event of my life that had caused a bad mark beside my name. Then, I watched myself erase each of those bad marks and place a mark beside one of my three parent's names as the person who had set me up to fail in the first place. *Who could I have been, if I had been raised by healthy parents? I can only wonder what my life could have been like, if that had happened.*

Two months later, Betty set up a Healing Retreat for any of her female patients who wanted to attend. At the end of the three days, she spoke to us and asked that we make a poster of the issues we have had in the past and other things that affected us. Below are pictures of part of the posters I made at the end of Betty's Healing Retreat.

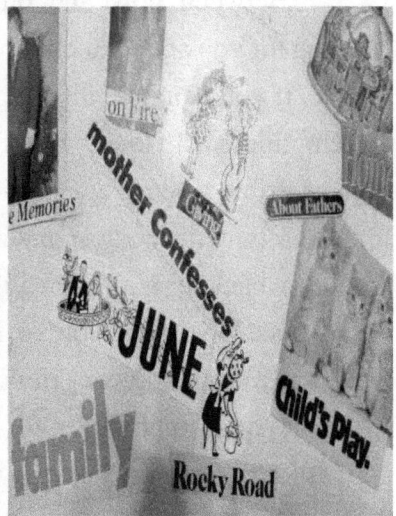

Debbie's Posters Made at Betty's Healing Retreat

13

≈

I'm Sick & Tired of Being Sick & Tired

It felt as if I was living and breathing in slow-motion for many weeks after my grieving process began. Each day, I was merely going through the required motions of my complicated life.

A month later, I ran across Bertie Catchings card, called her and made an appointment for a second reading. I had only seen her once back on June 23, 1985. She was the psychic who originally told me to write this book.

I sat across from Bertie at her small table. This time, she used a large crystal ball for my reading. "You have been a basket case lately and felt as if you were eighty-years-old. Since I last saw you, there were many medical problems and psychological problems. Your therapist is a God-send for you."

"As a child, you needed a lot of imagination to survive."

"When you write your second book, your daughter will find out about it. She will be excited and take it as a sign to write her own book about being victimized."

"Something needs to be written by your therapist for the book which tells about you when you first came to see her."

"This is a true story. Make it flow from your viewpoint in some chapters. You must speak for yourself in the book. Be sure to co-mingle the family throughout the pages."

"I see Europe, Canada and somewhere across the Pacific in your future. They are somehow connected with your book."

"Bertie, will Bart do more time?"

"He will for a burglary and other crimes. *I see many guns, and big money involved.* Be glad you got rid of him."

She reached for my right hand. "You have a theatrical line from your life line back toward your little finger. You are a brilliant person and well liked. Your marriages registered on your hand as affairs instead of marriages. You will live to be ninety. The hurt you are feeling now will go. You will never hurt as much as you do at this minute ever again."

I handed her money. She stood up and walked me to her front door. "God be with you, my dear!" She hugged me goodbye. It was the last time I ever saw her. In 2015, I ran across her obituary. Bertie left this Earth on *November 12, 2011.*

✳ ✳ ✳

On May 17, 1991, my first Supervised Visitation with Daniel and his dad, Oscar, began. Steve brought Daniel to my home promptly at two p.m. Daniel and I waited and waited for Oscar. He finally arrived one hour and thirty minutes late and didn't bother to call, so I looked at him with a frown. "Did you have car trouble?"

"No, I was working."

I drove them to a nearby video station, so that Daniel could play video games. Afterward, we stopped at an ice cream shop, and then, I drove them back to my home.

When Steve returned to pick up Daniel, he was curious. "How did it go today?"

"It was fine, except Oscar failed to call and was very late."

"Did you take notes?"

"I'll document every visit." I hugged Daniel and they left.

✳ ✳ ✳

The next week was Crystal's birthday. I decided to give her a special gift at her party that Steve had planned at their home on Saturday. When I arrived, I handed her a blue envelope and a small wrapped box. She received many nice gifts. Each of the kids drew a birthday card for her. Steve let each of them pick out a gift.

Then, she looked at me. "Now for Mom's gift."

"I hope you like it, honey."

Crystal read her card, opened the small box and frowned at what was inside. "Isn't this your ring, Mom?"

"It is, but many years ago I had that dome ring made and asked the jeweler to put the diamonds, from my wedding ring your dad gave me, in it. I thought you might like to have it."

"That's nice."

The tone of her voice told me she wasn't the least bit impressed. *Had I known then what she would do with my ring many years later, I would never have given it to her.*

When I got home from Crystal's party, my message light was flashing. I listened to it. "Hi, goodlookin', I just walked out of Club Fed. My brother, Pete, is here to help me pack up and move to Oregon where he lives. When I get settled in, I'll call you." *Bart is worse than a bad penny. He just keeps on showing up again and again.*

Thirty minutes later, my phone rang. I hesitated to answer. I was surprised to hear George's voice. "Debbie, I'd like to take you to supper tomorrow night."

"No, I'm not dating right now. Thanks anyway."

✳ ✳ ✳

The next morning, I received an unexpected visit from Steve. "Crystal, Adam Gentry and Kay Marie are on their way here. She told me this morning that she plans to leave me again. This will be the *third time, and it will be the last!*"

Crystal knocked and came in with Kay Marie and Adam Gentry. I looked at them and saw that Adam had a patch over his left eye. "What happened to Adam's eye?"

"Mom, he's quite a little scrapper. He got into a fight and had to have stitches."

"He takes after me, doesn't he?"

Crystal ignored my comment. She sat down with both kids, as Steve resumed his conversation. "In Crystal's mind, she's already single. I feel the sorriest for Daniel."

"I agree with you about Daniel."

Steve continued, "Plus, she almost aborted Adam Gentry."

"Mom, Steve and I are going to talk with Betty together. Will you watch the kids for us?"

"Certainly."

They left in a hurry. I decided to entertain the kids by letting them play dress-up. I helped Adam dress like a pirate, so he'd get over being embarrassed about his eye patch. Kay Marie dressed in my cowboy boots, sunglasses and a hat with a ponytail. I took their pictures because they looked so adorable. Then, we went out front, and I let them blow bubbles. Afterward, they came in to watch cartoons.

Three hours later, Crystal returned to pick up the kids.

"How did your visit with Betty go?"

"It was a lot tougher with Steve there. Betty asked me a question. 'If I could choose, at what age and position would I like to be?' "

I smiled at the familiar question from Betty.

"I picked eight, before Bart showed up. She asked me to start writing down my feelings. Steve is going to see Betty alone to work on his problems of control and abandonment. She told us there were reasons why we each chose the other to marry. It just didn't happen."

I thought back in time. *Crystal at eight years of age would be the year before I married Bart.*

Unexpectedly, Crystal surprised me. "The John Bradshaw book titled, *The Family,* is a good book."

"Honey, you and Steve are working with the perfect psychotherapist. Betty knows how to decipher family issues and secrets better than anyone I've ever met."

✻ ✻ ✻

That weekend, I called Stacy. "Hi, I'd like to see your new apartment today and also the club you're managing. Is this a good day?"

"Sure. Come to my apartment first."

I arrived thirty minutes later. Stacy was living in a nice neighborhood. I was impressed with his new apartment. Then, I followed him in my car to visit the gay bar that he was now managing. When I parked beside the two-story, renovated house in the Gay District, I saw a flashing sign; *The Cockpit.*

Stacy waited for me at the side door.

I grinned. "Hey, that's a great name for a bar."

"It sure is. Wish it had been my idea. It's been here for ten years. Come inside, and I'll show you around."

Inside the club, he introduced me to his bartender and the DJ. Next, I met his boss, Rory. He stood up. "My goodness, Stacy didn't tell me how attractive you are."

I laughed. "He's very protective of me."

Stacy toured me through the club. "I've come up with new ideas to bring in customers every night. On Monday, we have a sing-along to Broadway shows. There is also Amateur Night on Tuesday. During our Movie Night on Wednesday, we show X-rated movies that you can't see, Mom. Our competitor next door has lost a lot of business since I took over."

"That doesn't surprise me one bit. You've always been so innovative, even when you were little."

"Friday night, I'm starting *Two Dollar Drink Special Night*."

"I'd like to come to one of the sing-alongs to the Broadway shows night, or is it too risqué for me to be here?"

"While the sing-along is happening, it would be okay for you to come. After it ends, I don't want you to be here because things change. You know what I mean."

"Yes, I do."

I smiled as I left. *My son respects me and that pleases me.*

✳ ✳ ✳

It was time for my next appointment with Betty. As usual, I updated her on what had transpired since our last visit.

"Debbie, I want to walk you back to your two recurring nightmares, your mother's indifference toward you, her lack of love or parenting, and your obvious sexual addition. I have come to the conclusion that there is a high possibility that *you were sexually abused by your dad.*"

I sat there in stunned silence. *That's strange. I don't recall my dad sexually abusing me when I was little.*

"I want you to get your mother alone the next time you see her. Pick a place where she can't run off and confront her about it. Tell her you need to know the truth."

"Do you honestly believe that may have happened to me?"

"Absolutely, I do. The signs are there."

I shook my head. "I can't believe it."

"You may be surprised by her response."

When I left Betty's office, her request kept whirring, non-stop through my brain. *Ask my mother if I was sexually abused by my dad? That can't be right.*

✳ ✳ ✳

That Saturday, Stacy dropped by. "Mom, I have some big news. Rory likes how I turned his club around so much that he wants to make me his partner and start a second bar."

"Did Rory give you a raise to go with your new title?"

"Yes, he did. It's twice what he was paying me."

"Wow, I'm impressed, but I have one question. Is working in a bar going to jeopardize your sobriety?"

"Not as long as I attend my AA meetings and keep on working with my Sponsor."

"That's all I wanted to know, then go for it!"

Suddenly, my doorbell rang. I went to see who it was and found Mother and Harry had arrived unexpectedly. I led them to the den. After they sat down, and I turned to Stacy. "Will you visit with Harry while I go to my bank? I need to make a deposit."

"Sure I will."

"Mother, why don't you join me? We won't be gone long, and then we can all go eat together."

She was eager to go. She stood up and walked to my patio door. "Momma, let me get my purse and keys from the bedroom."

I scurried down the hall, grabbed my purse and returned to the den. I casually led her out the backdoor, around the pool to the driveway gate and unlocked my car door for her. We got inside my Firebird; I backed out and drove about six blocks to my bank. Once there, I pulled into a long line at a drive-up window.

I knew it was time. I took a deep breath and turned to Mother. "Can I ask you something?"

"What is it?"

"When we lived on Hill Street, and I was two and my baby bed was in the same room that you and my dad slept in, did he sexually abuse me?" You would have thought the world had just ended. Mother froze. She didn't respond.

"Mother, I need the truth. Did he?" She remained motionless for the longest time.

Finally, while staring straight ahead instead of at me, she replied. "Yes, he did, but I will never speak about it again."

"And you did nothing to stop him to protect me?"

Her mouth puckered. *"No, and I'm sorry, but never ask me again."*

"I needed the truth. Thank you for giving me the truth."

There was nothing but silence between us, as I waited for a teller to help me. I drove us home and parked. We walked inside in silence. Mother approached Harry. "I don't feel good. We need to go back home, so I can lie down." They left without another word.

Stacy looked at me. "Did she get sick in your car or something?"

"Oh, it's probably one of her dizzy spells. How about I take you out to eat?"

"Let's go."

✳ ✳ ✳

Early the next morning, I phoned my brother, Matt. He answered his phone. "Hi, I have an important question for you."

"What's that, Sis?"

"When I was very little, and we lived on Hill Street, and there was no door on the bedroom where Mother and my dad slept, and my baby bed was beside their double window, did you hear my dad sexually abusing me?" *My voice broke midway through the long sentence.*

I waited a long time for his reply. "Yes, I could hear it. My bed was in the next room near their doorway. I honestly wanted to stop him, but I was only fifteen and not very big. I knew he would hurt me, so I didn't help you. I'm ashamed for letting you down. That's why I ran off, lied to get into the Air Force about my age and ended up in the Korean War. Your dad terrified me, but that's no excuse for not helping you. Can you forgive me?"

I whimpered, as tears flooded my cheeks. My voice grew more childlike. "I just wish someone had told me. I had no way to know. All I remember are the horrible nightmares about some man outside that double window beside my baby bed about to come in to get me, or a huge gorilla or elephant would chase me down the street. Those frightening images never made any sense to me. It took my psychotherapist to finally figure things out. *I feel so violated, and I never knew... and no one ever helped me."*

14

≈

Even Comic Heroes Have Bad Days

Oscar's fifth visit was coming up on Saturday. During our previous visit, he repeatedly attempted to get Daniel alone to talk with him. I made certain that it never happened.

I knew I was scheduled to attend an AFL-CIO meeting on Saturday, so I phoned Oscar. "Hi, I have a conflict this Saturday and will be out of town. Would you like to see Daniel the next Sunday from one to five p.m.?"

"I need to call my lawyer, and then I'll call you back."

❋ ❋ ❋

Instead, Oscar phoned Crystal and upset her, so Steve called him back. "Look, you hurt Daniel, and he's afraid of you."

Oscar snarled, "I don't believe you."

"Just a minute." He put Daniel on the phone.

"Dad, I'm afraid of you. I *never* want to be alone with you again."

"Steve made you say that, didn't he?" Daniel hung up.

❋ ❋ ❋

Oscar phoned me back. "Hey bitch, you're going to Hell, and your son is a gay, sexual pervert."

I hung up on him. He phoned back and left a long, ugly message. "Yeah, I seen your son's profile online and almost threw up. Nice product you sowed there. You've always been a selfish, unicorn loving, carnal lady with your psychics, horoscopes and whatever else you do. Until you come to the truth and not think queers are born that way and take responsibility for your actions, you'll spend your eternity in Hell. I know the truth about you. You'll say that I cussed you and hit your grandson. You're the one that does that, not me!"

I phoned Steve and repeated the vulgar message Oscar left on my voicemail. "Steve, until he settles down, I will have to find someone to accompany me during his visits with Daniel."

"Absolutely! The man has a loose screw. Save that message, in case my attorney wants to hear it."

✳ ✳ ✳

My out-of-town trip was so relaxing and exactly what I needed. After my election as Union President, I wrote a monthly newsletter titled *The Dispatch*. It was mailed out to all of our members and retirees. To my surprise, one of the retiree's wives, Mrs. Audrey R., had entered my newsletter in the State AFL-CIO Publications Contest. When they called out my name as the winner, she was sitting beside me and elbowed my side. "You better stand up, gal. You just won the First Place Award for Excellence in Writing."

I was stunned. "How could that happen? I didn't enter it."

"No, but I did it for you, now get on over there and get your beautiful plaque. You earned it."

The moment totally blew me away. I received a large wooden plaque with a burnt-edged piece of thin sheet metal with my name on it. I smiled at the audience. "Thank you to everyone, and a big thank you to Mrs. Audrey R. I'm so happy and honored!"

A week later, I was again surprised when one of the former Local Presidents presented me a smaller plaque for *Outstanding Leadership as President of the Local Union.*

✶ ✶ ✶

I drove home the following day from the two-day meeting. When I rolled my suitcase inside my back door, the den phone was ringing.

"Ms. Austin, I'm the Court Appointed Therapist for Daniel. I've read your notes about the vulgar comments that Oscar made to you. I would like your opinion about his treatment of Daniel."

"I am concerned that Oscar refuses to give his son a Christmas gift; he has terrible interaction with Daniel; Daniel tells me that he is afraid of his dad; Oscar drinks a lot, has a bad temper and physically abuses my grandson; he also refuses to feed Daniel when he's hungry."

"Thank you for that insight. I plan to visit with Daniel and Oscar tomorrow. I will confront Oscar about each of your concerns."

✶ ✶ ✶

I barely hung up when the phone rang.

"Debbie, this is Harry."

Instantly, I knew something was wrong. Harry has never phoned me. "What's going on?"

"Momma was at the beauty shop today under a hairdryer and got ill. Her hairdresser had to help her walk home, since her shop was just around the corner."

"But what happened?"

"She told me it felt like her head suddenly disappeared. She couldn't feel anything where her head should be."

"Did you take her to the doctor?"

"Yes, he gave her some heart medicine and wants her to get some rest."

"I'll call Crystal and tell her, and then I'll drive up there. I'm glad you're only 95 miles away." I hung up and phoned Crystal.

"Something happened to Mother at her beauty shop today. Harry just called. Mother was under the hairdryer and suddenly, she felt like her head just disappeared."

❋ ❋ ❋

I bought Mother some purple flowers when I arrived in my hometown and then drove to her home. Harry opened their door. I hurried in and found her in bed with a wet rag across her eyes.

"Momma, how are you feeling?"

"Pretty good for someone who *lost her head.*"

"Can I get you anything?"

"Yeah, a new head!"

I laughed. "At least you haven't lost your sense of humor."

"Help me to the living room couch."

I did my best to sit Mother up and get her onto her feet. She held onto my arm, as I slowly guided her to the couch. She noticed the flowers I brought. "My favorite flowers."

An hour later, Crystal, Steve, and all four kids arrived. While they visited with her, I quizzed Harry about her condition.

Two hours later, I could see that Mother was tiring. "Why don't we take a few pictures and then let Mother get some rest?"

Daniel took a picture of everyone either sitting on the couch or the floor around Mother. Then, I took one so that Daniel could be in one of the group pictures. I helped Momma to her bed and kissed her cheek. "Call me if you need me."

❋ ❋ ❋

A week later, I phoned to check on Mother. She answered her phone. "I'm fine now. I'm taking medication, and my head has finally returned."

"That's great! I'm here anytime you need me. I love you!"

I hung up the phone. It rang and startled me.

"Sis, I need to tell you something. I already know about Mother. It isn't that. It's me."

"I hear a worried tone in your voice."

"Yeah, I went to see my doctor yesterday. He found several skin cancers on my face. I've been out in the sun too much playing golf without sunblock or a hat. I hadn't told you, but he had to deaden my face quite a few times today to remove many deep cancers from my cheekbone area. The latest ones were extremely deep. He told me I may need chemotherapy depending on the lab results. I want you to know, if it comes to that, I won't take chemo. Whatever happens, will happen. I wanted to be the one to tell you, just in case."

"I understand how you feel. That decision belongs to you. I pray it won't come to that. You know I love you a lot."

"And I love you, Sis."

I hung up. *Oh Lord, when it rains, it's a monsoon.*

✷ ✷ ✷

The next day at work, I must have had a worried look on my face. Johnny came up behind me and whispered, "Hi, pretty lady."

I recognized his voice. "Hello, my special friend." I turned around and smiled for the first time in days.

"You seem to have a lot on your mind today."

"Oh, does it show?"

"You could say that, but I bet I can get you to smile."

"Go for it!"

He gave my white skirt and purple blouse a once over. "I'll give you an A+ on your outfit today."

I smiled. "I can top that. The cologne you're wearing today is driving me crazy!" We both laughed and went to our separate work areas. *If only I had met Johnny before his wife did.*

✷ ✷ ✷

Stacy called me the next morning. "Mom, I want your advice about a Travel Agent. She claims I owe her money. I made a $500 *deposit on a trip, couldn't get the time off, and I wrote her a letter requesting a refund.* She just called and claimed I didn't give her proper notice. She's going to have me arrested."

"Send her a Certified Letter requiring a signature. Tell her she is committing fraud, and she must refund your money immediately, or you will report her to the State Attorney General for *Business Fraud.*"

"She won't care. She's a hateful bitch!"

"Try it and see. I bet it works."

"Okay, but she'll probably try to get me arrested anyway."

✳ ✳ ✳

A week later, I dropped by The Cockpit to see Stacy. When I walked in the side door, he hurried toward me. "Your idea worked! She sent me a refund check today. I want to buy you lunch anywhere you like."

"How about Casa Bonita?"

"Let's go." I followed Stacy outside to his Mustang. On the way, he turned to me. "I want to ask you something at lunch."

"I hope it's more good news."

After we were seated at a table in Casa Bonita, he smiled. "Would I make a good model?"

"You certainly turn heads with your looks, and I can see that you've been lifting weights lately. Is it for a clothes magazine?"

"No, it's for a men's magazine. Gay men, of course."

"Well, I can't see the harm in that. Be sure and get me a copy when it gets released."

He didn't reply. He just flashed a quick smile, which usually meant he hadn't told me everything.

✳ ✳ ✳

Unfortunately, it was almost time for my next Supervised Visitation on Saturday with Daniel and Oscar. I phoned a dancing friend, Chuck M., and explained my recent problem with Oscar.

He said, "Of course, I will accompany you and little Daniel while you're dealing with that creep for four hours."

True to his word, Chuck showed up in his big black BMW. Oscar was a bit uncomfortable riding in such a fine car. Then, he made a request. "Can you drive me by my cousin's trailer? He has something he wants to give to Daniel."

Chuck smiled. "I will gladly do it with directions."

After we arrived, we waited in Chuck's car while Oscar went inside. Our wait grew longer and longer. Finally, I got out and knocked on the trailer door. Oscar yanked it open. "Yeah, yeah. Don't be so pushy. I'm visitin' with my cuz'."

Oscar finally rejoined us in Chuck's car. He handed Daniel an armful of comic books. Daniel was on top of the world about it. Since I had endured a huge issue with Crystal recently about a comic book and the *Robin Hood* movie, I could only hope that she had moved beyond her recent nonsense from her church.

Chuck and I talked, while Daniel and Oscar played video games for three hours. When Chuck dropped us off at my home, I hugged him. "I can't thank you enough for being with us today."

"Anytime, just let me know."

Daniel hugged his dad, and Oscar drove away. I kissed Daniel just as Crystal arrived to pick him up. He turned to Crystal, "Mommy, look what I got!"

When her eyes saw the stack of comic books in Daniel's arms, she went ballistic at me. "I told you, no comic books for him!"

"Stop right there. I had nothing to do with it. Take it up with Oscar. His cousin gave them to him for Daniel."

"Why didn't you tell him to keep them?"

"Because I see nothing wrong with them. Apparently, you do, so take it up with Oscar."

Crystal took Daniel and left in a huff. Later, Steve called me after she brought Daniel home. "She and Oscar had a screaming match over the phone. Afterward, *she destroyed Daniel's comic books in a trashcan fire in our alley.*"

"Steve, you know as well as I do that there was *nothing* wrong with any of those comic books. When is this idiocy going to stop? I am concerned for Crystal. Her depression fits are growing more and more dangerous. Depression runs in my family, but I assure you that I am no longer a victim of depression, thanks to Betty T."

Steve shocked me with his next comment. *"I am concerned that Crystal is talking to you. I feel I am being set up in Crystal's eyes as the abuser."*

"From my viewpoint, most of her abuse came from Bart, but I have witnessed loud arguments between the two of you. The ones that stand out were when Stacy and I ate dinner at your home. You and Crystal got into a huge argument in front of us and your children about how the peas should be eaten and where the silverware should be placed. The other time, Stacy and I met you two at a famous restaurant for lunch. Suddenly, a big argument broke out, after you publicly scolded Crystal about how she handled her checkbook and check register. I was embarrassed for my daughter."

"Betty told me that I'm in a *Lose-Lose* situation with Crystal. If I help her, I lose; if I don't, I lose. She asked me to make a list of the common attractions between my three wives. There aren't any, as I see it. She also wants me to list what Crystal and I have in common. *I feel it's very little."*

"Steve, Betty always has good reasons for asking us to do a more internal search of our feelings and choices."

"She got me to talk about my family role as the caretaker; my mom's alcoholism and my dad's abandonment of me and Will, one of my brothers. Growing up, Will and I talked things out together. My drunk of a Mother called me night before last. Honestly, I believe my marriage to Crystal is finally over."

"Please don't be too hasty. I know you are hurt and confused. Give it just a little more time for the kids."

When am I going to get a rest from all of this family insanity? I feel as if I'm living in a minefield, and I never know when the next explosion will hit me.

✽ ✽ ✽

On Mother's Day, 1992, I phoned Crystal. "Would you like to join me this weekend? I'm going to go see Mother and surprise her for Mother's Day."

"Yeah, I'd like to do that."

Finally, some positive words from my daughter.

We had a pleasant drive to my hometown. I stopped by a store so we could buy Mother some red roses and a card. I parked beside Mother's home. Crystal got out and knocked on their door, then we went inside and surprised her with the roses and her card. Mother quickly put her vase of roses on a living room table along with our card. Suddenly, she turned around with a funny look. "Debbie, your father's in town. He called me ten minutes ago. He wants to see you."

"He can't possibly know I'm here. This can't be happening!"

Her phone rang five minutes later. "Yes, she and Crystal just arrived to surprise me for Mother's Day."

After she hung up, I shook my head. "Why did you say that?"

"Because he wants to see you and put you in his will."

"Call him back and tell him not to come. *I want nothing from the man who put my young daughter into a tub of hot water to punish her years ago.*"

"He didn't give me his phone number."

"That's just great!"

My dad knocked on Mother's front door twenty minutes later. Harry stood up and went out the backdoor. I walked into their kitchen and closed the door. Crystal stayed with Mother, while she let my dad and his young grandson inside her home."

I never want to see that rotten SOB again as long as I live.

That's the one thing that Mother actually *did* teach me, as I was growing up. "Never say never, because never is a long time."

Sure enough, she opened the kitchen door. "Your dad doesn't want to leave, until he sees you for a few minutes."

"No, Mother!"

"He has his young grandson with him. He'd like to meet you. He told me he's heard a lot about you."

I threw my hands up. "Okay, but he better not mention anything about his will."

I followed Mother to her living room. My dad jumped to his feet and put his eight-year-old grandson in front of him. "Debbie, meet my grandson, Doug."

"It's nice to meet you, young man."

I could see some of the same terror in the youngster's eyes that I had in my eyes when I was growing up around my dad. My heart went out to him. *It is horrible that this monster, and so-called father of mine, now has his hands on yet another young child.*

"How are my two half-brothers, Roger and Kent, doing?"

"Kent got married and had Doug. They got into drugs, left Doug with us and vanished. We haven't heard from them in years. Roger just graduated from college and is looking for a job."

None of that surprises me. My dad wasn't fond of Kent, when I was briefly around them. He rode the poor boy extremely hard, and he always favored Roger. (That is the last time I ever saw my dad. He has since passed away. Maybe, in time, I can forgive him for abusing me, my brother and Crystal. I feel certain that he also physically abused Kent.)

Doug and my dad, "The Abuser"

15

≈

Never Say Never

"Doug, you remind me a lot of your dad."

He smiled. "That's what I've heard."

"Debbie, if you wouldn't mind, I'd like for you to take a picture of me with Crystal and Doug."

"Okay." I went to Mother's bedroom to get my camera, came back and snapped their picture.

He turned to Crystal. "If you give me your mailing address, I'll write you a letter."

Crystal jotted down her address on a piece of paper and handed it to him. I kept my distance from him. It was hard to look at him. He finally said, "We need to go. It's a long drive home."

They left as swiftly as they arrived. After Mother closed her front door, I looked at Crystal. "Mark my words. *He will never write to you.*"

Mother made one of her sour-faced looks, as if I had to be wrong.

I couldn't decide which emotion inside of me was the greatest at that moment, my anger at my dad or sympathy for little Doug. My prediction that Crystal would never hear from my dad was right-on-target. It never happened.

✳ ✳ ✳

Thankfully, my next visit with Betty was only two days later. She spotted my look of extreme distress, the moment I sat down across from her.

"Looks like we have a lot to discuss today."

"That's the truth. I did as you asked and confronted Mother about the possibility of my dad abusing me in my baby bed, and I asked her *why she didn't help me.* I also confronted my brother, Matt, because he lived with us back then. Both of them admitted that you were correct. I received a brief apology from each of them."

"How do you feel to finally know the truth about your past?"

"I'm not angry at Mother or Matt, but I am disappointed."

"Let's talk about that. Tell me your disappointment."

"Had it been me and Crystal's dad had sexually abused her when she was only two-years-old, I would have gone to the police and then divorced him. That is exactly what I did, when I found that white satchel."

"Can you see how your mother set you up once again?"

"Oh yes, and it makes me tired just to think about all the ways she has let me down. It's no wonder I quickly developed such an explosive temper as a young child." I shook my head and fought back my tears. "I never had a chance, did I?"

"Not until you decided to find a way to help yourself."

"It's my belief that God sent that *Whispering Angel* to me back in 1981, so that I would eventually be sitting right here today."

"I completely agree. You will no longer be a victim. You are learning to keep your responses on an even keel, instead of that constant rollercoaster of anger that you were riding."

Next, I went over the other key moments from my past two weeks, including my dad's recent surprise visit at Mother's house.

"What feelings popped up as a result of seeing him again?"

"Raging anger swept through me. I wanted to choke him."

"Which memory triggered that feeling?"

"It was a combination. The latest anger came when I learned about his sexual abuse of me when I was only two-years-old, and that's why I wanted to choke him."

"Was there another reason why you wanted to choke him?"

"Yes, it was the first time I had seen him since 1965. He and his wife put Crystal into a tub of hot water to punish her."

"The good news is that *truth holds the power of healing.* Before our next visit, I want you to journal what happened to Crystal, how you reacted, and the result. Bring it with you next time, so that we can talk about it."

✳ ✳ ✳

After that visit, I needed some fun to relax. I attended another Methodist Singles outing. George Austin showed up again and sat beside me. "When are you going to go out with me?"

"I'm not sure."

"At least let me take you out to dinner tomorrow night. You might discover that I'm a nice guy."

"Okay, dinner sounds good. What time?"

"I'm always prompt. Eight o'clock, but I need your address and phone number." I jotted both of them on a napkin and handed it to him.

He beamed. "Perfect!"

The next night, he was right on time and arrived with a bouquet of pink flowers and a huge smile. He drove us to an expensive restaurant and treated me like a queen all evening. Before we left, he took my right hand. "I'm going on a short trip in two weeks. Come go with me."

"If it's business, you'll be busy, and I'd get bored."

"It's an outdoor event. You'll meet many interesting guys."

"As long as you get me a separate hotel room, I'll go."

"You got it, lady."

✳ ✳ ✳

Stacy's friend, Danny S., phoned me again. "Debbie, I bet you don't know what Stacy is doing these days."

"Yes, I do. He's co-owner of The Cockpit, lifting weights, and he's modeling for a gay magazine. Has it come out yet?"

"It came out several weeks ago. I'm sure he hasn't given you a copy."

"What's the name of the magazine?"

"I'd better not tell you. Why don't you ask him?"

"Okay, I will."

The tone in Danny's voice told me that Stacy was up to something, and I may not like it.

✳ ✳ ✳

Before I went to work the next day, I paid Stacy a surprise visit at his apartment. I knew what time he usually left for work at The Cockpit, so I rang his doorbell. He opened his door. "Mom, this is unexpected. Come on in."

I followed him into his living room and noticed a colorful picture on his computer screen. He quickly walked in front of his computer and turned it off.

"Who was in that picture?"

"Oh, no one you know."

"No one? *No one* looks my son."

"It was a friend of mine. It's a guy thing."

Stacy was a bundle of nerves. I knew he wasn't telling me the truth. "Has that magazine you told me about come out yet?"

"Yeah, but I don't have a copy of it right now."

"When are you going to tell me what you're really doing?"

"I don't know what you mean?"

"Did I stutter? What are you really doing?"

"Like I said, you aren't going to like hearing this, Mom."

"I'll be the judge of that. Let's hear the truth."

"It's a men's magazine. I'm not wearing much."

"In that picture I saw, there weren't any clothes."

His lips tightened. "You're right. It was me, but there is a flag draped over, you know where."

"I'm sure I have a good idea about 'you know where.' "

I waited and waited. "Okay, it's a porn magazine. I'm on the cover. It's called, *This Week in The South.* Not many models ever make a cover." He nervously awaited my reaction.

"I don't know what to say. I've never thought of my son as a porn star."

"Are you mad at me?"

"Honestly, I don't know what I'm feeling or what to say. It's a shock, that's for sure. Wow!" I shook my head.

Stacy sort of froze and continued to wait for my reaction.

"I need some time to think about this. Boy, if your dad and the family find out! It's a lot to swallow. I have to leave, or I'll be late for work."

I sat in my car for the longest time in stunned silence. *I need to talk to Betty about this one.*

✻✻✻

To accept the Porn Star status for Stacy is much harder for me than the gay issue. Stacy didn't choose to be gay, but he is choosing to be involved in porn. It's a lot to consider and an extremely huge step. There will be no turning back for him. He will always be remembered as a porn star.

My mind couldn't wrap itself around Stacy's porn world. And to think, I have yet to confide in even one friend that Stacy is gay, much less that he's now involved in porn. I have no doubt that the more porn he does, the greater the issues will become. I drove to work and prayed for a solution.

✳ ✳ ✳

Steve phoned me that night after I got home from work. "Crystal mailed out 30 resumes today. The last time she was going to leave us, I called in that Church on the Rock group to talk to her. After they had her for four hours, she was *re-convinced* to stay with me."

Steve's news made me f'ing furious. It sounds like brainwashing! I worked hard not to explode at him for doing that to Crystal. How dare he be in cahoots with that crazy Church on the Rock group and approve of them brainwashing my daughter, just to keep her from leaving him. It feels like he just made a veiled threat that he'll call them in again.

"Steve, if Crystal asks me not to talk to you anymore, I won't. My mom is very depressed over all of this, and I don't want you to call and upset her."

"My folks don't know either."

"Look, why not give it some time and let Crystal work with Betty? Don't push her. She doesn't really know what she wants."

✳ ✳ ✳

Steve phoned me the next morning. "Crystal asked me if I talked to you yesterday. I told her 'No.' Will you go along with me on this?"

"No, I won't lie for you, and I wish you had told her the truth instead."

"She told me that Betty encouraged her not to make any decisions right now about a job." *Clearly Steve doesn't want Crystal to go to work. He wants her to be a stay-at-home-mom.*

"I need to get ready for work, Steve."

I hung up and called Betty. I got her answering machine, so, I left her a message. "Betty, I'm concerned that *Steve just asked me to lie to Crystal.* I told him I won't do that. Crystal has been understandably depressed. I'm also concerned that Steve previously called in that crazy church to control Crystal's decisions and now, it sounds as if he just threatened to do it again."

I hung up and my busy phone rang. My caller ID said it was Crystal. "Mom, Bart just called me. He got married yesterday to a nice lady named Connie in Oregon."

"That's makes number four for him. He's one ahead of me."

"He sounds extremely happy."

"Let's hope he can finally stay out of trouble with *Johnny Law*. Does she have any children?"

"Yes, she has two girls."

"That's not good."

"Talk to you later, Mom." She hung up. I looked at my calendar. They were married on June 22, 1992. *How touching! My ex calls my daughter, who claims Bart destroyed her life, to tell her he got married. It sounds like she enjoyed telling me that news in a somewhat sadistic sort of way. Her ongoing, friendly relationship with Bart tells me that I'm still in the dark about a lot of things, and I probably won't like any of them.*

When I hung up, my message light was on, so I listened to it. "Debbie, got your message. I honor your decision not to keep a secret. That's what keeps us sick. If it upsets Crystal to hear the truth, that's what is supposed to happen. I will phone her back as quickly as possible, if she calls my office." *All the more reason why I'm so glad my Al-Anon Sponsor found Betty for me to work with.*

✳ ✳ ✳

Time for another Supervised Visitation soon rolled around. I called Stacy. "Would you do a big favor for me and come over here during Oscar's visit tomorrow?"

"Sure, Mom."

Crystal brought Daniel to my home the next day and saw Stacy sitting on the couch. He waved at her.

She looked at Stacy. "I haven't seen you in a while."

"It wasn't my doing. It was yours."

"Mom, can you bring Daniel half-way home after Oscar's visit? We have church plans tonight."

"Okay, I can do that."

She gave Daniel a hug and quickly left before Oscar arrived. Thirty minutes later, he had yet to show up. "Daniel, would you phone your dad and see when he'll be here?"

Daniel made the call, hung up and tugged on my arm. "Nana, he'll be here in five minutes."

"Thank you, sweetheart."

Finally, Oscar arrived and knocked on the door. All three of us met him at the door. "We're ready to go."

Daniel and Oscar piled into my Firebird. Stacy followed us in his car. We parked our cars and went inside. Oscar and Daniel played video games beside each other for three hours. Stacy also played some games across the room. I kept an eye on Oscar the whole visit. Later, Stacy sat down. "Mom, I need to go."

"Okay. Thanks so much for being here today."

After Stacy left, Oscar took Daniel to the food area, bought him some ice cream and whispered something to him. I watched Daniel approach the Video Machine Manager and talk to him. When he turned around, I could see that he was holding a big cup full of video coins.

Daniel and Oscar sat down at my table. I was steamed. "Daniel, how did you end up with all of those new video coins?"

He looked sheepish and dropped his head. "My dad told me to tell him that I lost ten coins when his machine malfunctioned."

I scolded Oscar. *"Don't you dare tell my grandson to lie like that again, or I will see you in court myself!"*

Oscar swelled up. "It ain't non-ah your business, bitch!"

"Don't be so sure about that, mister. I'm working with Steve's attorney, and I make reports to the court on your visit behavior with Daniel."

From the look on Oscar's face, you would have thought I had shot him. He didn't say another word all the way home.

When I met Crystal half-way, I got out of my car and told her what Oscar did and my reaction. She grinned. "Better you than me. I would have been screaming at him!"

"Would you like to visit Stacy at his new job sometime? I think it's time you two started talking again."

"Okay. Let me know when."

"Tomorrow at noon works for me."

"I'll pick you up at eleven a.m., Mom."

✳ ✳ ✳

Crystal showed up promptly at eleven in her SUV. She drove us downtown to Stacy's club, *The Cockpit*, and parked beside it. When we got out and headed to the side door, she stopped. "What do you think Stacy will say when he sees me, Mom?"

"He'll be thrilled to death that you came to see him at work."

We went inside, and I approached the bartender. "Would you call Stacy on your telephone? I'm his mom and we're here to surprise him."

The bartender called Stacy. When he walked toward us and saw Crystal, he was grinning from ear-to-ear and stunned that Crystal actually walked into a gay bar because he was the manager."

He smiled, "Welcome to *The Cockpit,* Sis."

She smiled. "This is quite a layout. I like it."

Stacy toured us through the entire, two-story bar and showed us the outside balcony overlooking a busy street.

"Crystal, my club is now the *Number One Gay Bar* in town. When I took over, it was only number six."

"It's quite impressive."

"Let me take both of you to see my new condo?"

I was shocked. "When did this happen, Stacy?"

"My AA friend that you met named Richard H. lives in the building. He told me that I could buy a condo in a Sheriff's Sale on the courthouse steps. He even loaned me the money."

"I'm happy for you, honey! It's a place to call your own."

Stacy drove us six blocks and pointed. "There it is on the second floor of that building to your left. Want to take a guided tour?"

We replied, "Certainly!"

Stacy stopped in his parking spot. Then, he led us through a gate and upstairs to his door. He toured us through his two-story condo, complete with two bedrooms and two balconies.

Crystal smiled. "I love it!"

Next, we had lunch, and then Stacy drove us to his club to get Crystal's SUV.

On the way to my home, Crystal asked, "Has Steve been talking to you about us?"

"Yes, and he asked me to lie to you about it, but I refused."

"Honestly, I've been talking to an old high school friend for the last year and have realized how unhappy I am." *I feel certain it has to be Eric, because he was always so crazy about her."*

✳ ✳ ✳

The following weekend, George picked me up. He drove us to a small town about three hours away. When we arrived, he parked near what appeared to be some kind of a flea market. After we got out of his car and walked closer, I discovered I was wrong.

George led me along the middle path in the covered area. On each side of us were farriers shoeing horses or making new horseshoes on their anvils. It felt like I had just stepped back into the Old West days. One-by-one, George introduced me to each farrier. He seemed to be a legend to them. "Are you some kind of a celebrity here?"

He chuckled. "You could say that. I've been doing it for many years. I even invented an improved anvil. If you look closely, you'll see my name on most of those anvils."

Dinner that night was no ordinary event either. We got dressed up, and George walked me into a huge room filled with farriers and their wives or girlfriends. During the evening, an emcee stood up and presented him with a Farrier Plaque of Honor.

George sat down and showed me his plaque. I smiled at him. "How come you never mentioned this to me before?"

"I wanted to surprise you. Are you surprised?"

"You could say that."

After we left, he walked me to my hotel room and unlocked the door. I stepped inside and turned. "Goodnight, George."

He kissed me. "I'm crazy about you. Will you marry me?"

I shook my head. "No, I'm not ready to get married."

"Can I change your mind?"

"I doubt it."

✳ ✳ ✳

My next visit with Betty was due in three days. I had a lot of things I wanted to discuss with her by then.

I remembered what Oscar once mentioned about Stacy being online, so I decided to search the internet, but I found nothing about Stacy Malone anywhere. I phoned Stacy's friend who would keep me informed. "Hi, I've been trying to find Stacy online and can't. Do you have his internet name?"

"I don't think I should give it to you."

"Why not?"

"Because I don't want him mad at me. It's his porn site."

"Okay, then I'll call him and ask him myself."

I hung up and dialed Stacy. "Hi, what's your porn name?"

"Why do you want to know?"

"Oh, I thought I might look you up online."

"Are you sure you want to do that, Mom? There are pictures of me out there that I don't want you to see."

"Well, do you have a blog or something I can see?"

"I have a chat page where my fans ask me questions."

"And your porn name is?"

"Sawyer Stallion!"

It was time to find Stacy's Forum, or should I say, *Sawyer Stallion's Forum*. I did a name search and found it, but first I had to agree that I was over 18 and knew that some conversations and pictures could be about sexual material.

I quickly found a long list of men who had sent him questions on a wide range of subjects. *Now, it's time to put on my big girl boots and wade into this new world that my son has chosen.*

16

≈

Dad Issues Galore

I clicked on the question titled *Drugs and Alcohol,* from Anthony P.

"Sawyer, I saw that u quit all drugs and alcohol when u were young. Did you ever consider yourself an alcoholic?"

Stacy's answers were always, *From: Sawyer.* He gave a lengthy answer. "It took me a while to finally get into AA. I only kept going to meetings to keep my mom happy. I had a tough AA Sponsor who was *very smart.*"

Well that Q&A wasn't so bad. The other questions ranged from: suicide, goatees, your mother, unsafe sex, career choices, porn directors, music, coming out, the Gayvn Awards, the Grabby Awards, but the one from Mr. X caught my eye. Curiosity got the best of me. I clicked on the subject, Mr. X, to read what he wrote.

Mr. X posted: "I am a Hollywood actor, *very famous,* but I'm not into bragging. And yes, let's just say I'm *familiar* with one of the hottest young actors in film today (name deleted). I'm in the closet, so I'm Mr. X, but I have seen you Mr. Stallion. I am wanted by so many women, but I really want to be with a guy. My love life ain't exactly paradise, but, yeah, I've actually considered shocking America and doing a gay porno. But I love my career too much. Maybe one day, but whatever. PS I don't care who does or doesn't believe me. I just needed to vent."

Sawyer's reply to Mr. X: "I certainly believe you, and I am sure that it is tough to be so famous and live a life that does not allow you to express your sexuality because of everyone's *sex-pectations* of you. But you get to make the big bucks in the big productions, while I slave away to get myself into a top-rated studio's porn movie. It's good to know my work is appreciated by rich and famous people, too. Thanks!!! Sawyer."

Oh Lord, it sounds like he's already made some porn movies. I looked down his subject list and saw, *This Week in the South.* I clicked on the link and there was that picture that I accidentally saw on Stacy's computer the other day. When I got a closer look at the picture with a flag draped across his hip and privates, I could see that all of his body muscles suddenly looked enormous. *It must have taken tons of weightlifting to get his muscles that huge!* Reality slapped me in the face. *It doesn't matter whether I like it or not, my son is into gay porn in a big way.*

✳ ✳ ✳

I was floundering after that latest reality about Stacy. *Good grief, I can't talk to anyone about it, especially not Mother, Crystal or Lori.* I checked my calendar. My next appointment with Betty seemed eons away. My only port-in-a-storm was Johnny. When I walked into the lunchroom at work, he was sitting there alone at a lunch table. I sat down across from him, but he didn't say a word.

"Is something wrong?"

"Yes, very wrong."

"What's happened?"

"Someone phoned my boss in Los Angeles. He called me today with a warning. 'You can't talk to Debbie anymore at work.' "

"Why not?"

"Some nameless person accused us of having an affair."

I leaned back in disbelief. *"Well, I know that's not true."*

"So do I, but I'm barred from talking to you."

"Since when is *talking* an affair?"

"You know how some people can be."

"Yeah, they're jealous as hell of me. Any idea who did it?"

"Not a clue."

"This is awful timing. I'm dealing with something I never thought I'd ever have to face, and now, this garbage comes out of left field. I guess we just can't talk anymore, Johnny. I would never cost you your job."

"For a while we can't talk, that's how it has to be. I'm sorry."

"I understand, but if I ever find out who did this..."

He interrupted. "I'll be first in line, if a name ever surfaces."

✷ ✷ ✷

When I arrived at home that night, I realized that my next visit with Betty was the following morning. It was time to journal the last night I spent with my dad and his wife, Olive, when Crystal was only four. This is what I wrote for Betty about that awful time:

✷ ✷ ✷

"I worked nights at a phone company, when Crystal and I moved to Tennessee in 1965. We stayed with my dad, Olive and their boys, Roger and Kent. They asked me to pay weekly rent, buy my own groceries and help Olive with housecleaning and ironing. She was a stay-at-home mom. I was a working mom. The reason I moved there was because of an unfortunate affair. I felt that only distance would stop Dan from following me everywhere, so I quit my job, took Crystal and moved there.

At first, things seemed good with my dad and his family, but signs of trouble soon began to surface. I had a date with Tim one night. My dad didn't ask, *he demanded,* I break my date with Tim and take Kent and Roger to a party instead.

The next incident came a month later. I was off that night. I looked forward to spending time with Crystal. After supper, I washed dishes and sat in a chair. "Crystal, come and sit in Mommy's lap."

The moment she did, my dad and Olive grew enraged. He shouted, "You can't hold her anymore!"

"What are you talking about? She's my daughter!"

Olive informed me, "You are gone in the evenings. She's now *our little girl*, because we take care of her. You don't!"

"No, she's my daughter, and I will hold her if I want to!"

I stood up, grabbed Crystal by the hand and fled to our bedroom. Crystal looked upset. "Baby, how about I give you a bath right now?"

"No! I don't want to, Mommy."

"It will help you sleep tonight."

She whined a little bit and finally said, "Okay."

I grabbed her pajamas from our bedroom and one of the towels and a washrag I had to buy, because Olive wouldn't allow me to use their towels. I led Crystal into the bathroom, closed the door and locked it. After I ran some water, I undressed her and held both of her hands, while she stepped into the tub. As I began to put soap on her legs, she cried. "What's wrong, baby?"

"My bottom hurts."

"Stand up and let Mommy look."

The moment she stood up and turned, I went into shock. "What happened to you? Your little bottom and the back of your legs look scalded."

Crystal whimpered. *"Olive and Grandpa told me I was a bad girl and punished me in a tub of hot water. It hurts, Mommy!"*

Angry tears flowed down my cheeks. I quickly and gently washed Crystal, took her out of the tub, put her into her pajamas and tucked her into our bed. I closed our bedroom door and stormed into their den.

"Who do you two think you are? You scalded Crystal's bottom and legs! How dare you two do that to my daughter!"

This picture was taken when Debbie's dad and his wife bought her a birthday cake.

Two months later, they punished Crystal by putting her into a tub of scalding hot water. Only monsters would do that to a young child.

✱✱✱

Olive got in my face. "She's not yours anymore. She belongs to us."

"Dream on! I won't tolerate physical abuse to my child!"

My dad came at me. I stood my ground. "Stop right there! I'm not afraid of you anymore!"

"I can still whip you anytime I want. I'm a lot bigger than you. This is our home and our rules!"

"Crystal is my daughter. I discipline her. You don't!"

I scurried into our bedroom, locked the door and phoned Mother collect. I told her what had happened and asked for her help.

"Momma, I had to buy some furniture to live here. We must get out of here quick. My dad is crazy mean! Can you help us?"

"I'll drive all night and rent a U-Haul trailer when I arrive. Give me your phone number. I'll call you in the morning."

✱✱✱

I barely slept all night for fear my dad would charge into our room and hurt me or Crystal. When morning came, I stayed inside our room, until I heard my dad drive away. I opened the door and went to the kitchen to get some food I bought for Crystal and me to eat.

Olive charged toward me. "What do you think you're doing?"

"We're hungry. I bought this food, so we will eat it."

"Not in the bedroom, you won't!"

"You can't stop me!" I pushed past her, went into our bedroom and locked the door. Then, I dressed Crystal, and I got dressed. I kept looking out the window in our bedroom for any sign of Mother and the trailer, while I packed two suitcases.

A long hour crept past. Finally, I heard the house phone ring. Olive banged on my door. "Your Mother is on the phone."

"I'll take the call in my bedroom."

"Suit yourself!"

"Debbie, I'm almost there. Are you ready?"

"Yes." I hung up and carried one suitcase down the stairs into their basement and returned to our bedroom.

When I brought the other suitcase to the basement stairs door, Olive tried to block me. "You aren't going anywhere. I called your dad. He's on his way home to stop you!"

"Move out of my way!"

"You better not scratch my floor with your furniture!"

I took the second suitcase downstairs and rushed back up the stairs to our bedroom. I had purchased a chest of drawers and a radio. I quietly eased both of them toward our bedroom door. As I peered out our window, Mother drove up out front and parked with a U-Haul trailer. I took Crystal's hand. "Come with me, baby." When I opened our door, we stepped into the hall.

Olive screamed, "Your dad will hurt you. You'll be sorry!"

I ignored her, led Crystal down the stairs to the basement, opened their garage door, and took Crystal outside. Mother was waiting. "Put Crystal in your car. I have two suitcases." I ran to the garage and rolled both suitcases toward the U-Haul. Mother opened the trailer door. "I have two pieces of furniture we can't carry."

Frantically, I looked around and spotted a carpenter working on a new house across the street. I dashed toward him to explain my dilemma. "My Dad hurt my daughter. My mom drove all night to help me get out of his house. I'll give you twenty dollars to help me get two pieces of furniture down the basement stairs and into that U-Haul. My dad is on the way home to stop us!"

The carpenter didn't hesitate. "Let's go!"

We rushed across the street through the garage door, up the basement stairs and brought each piece down separately and loaded them into the trailer. I paid him. "You are a lifesaver!"

I hurried into the passenger seat of Mother's green Chevy. "Let's get out of here quick!" She stepped on the gas. The corner was only a half block away. As she slowed her car at the Stop Sign, I looked to my right. A dirt street dead-ended twenty feet to the right of the paved street where we were about to turn left to make our getaway.

Suddenly, I saw my dad's huge Chrysler fly into view airborne. It landed in the reddish dirt. Suddenly, it was like I was watching a slow motion movie. As his wheels touched down, the red dirt swirled all around his car wheels. His car bounced several times. He glared at me with a look of pure hatred. I gave him a *Go to Hell* stare and then pointed left. "Momma, turn the corner quick and get us out of here!"

"Betty, this is the reason why I wanted to choke my dad, when he showed up at Mother's house on Mother's Day recently!"

17

≈

Never a Dull Moment

The following day, I sat down across from Betty and handed her my written explanation about *why I wanted to choke my dad* the last time I saw him at Mother's home. I waited while she read each page and watched her face for reactions over various moments throughout the incident. For once, it was Betty who heaved a deep sigh after she read the final page. *"I'm so proud of you for reacting as sternly and suddenly as you did that day to your father's abuse of Crystal."*

"Just as I did the morning I found that white satchel and drove away with a ton of evidence against Bart and hid it. I have zero tolerance for abuse. I will stop it anyway I can. Look what I went through to protect Rhonda's children, and she was clearly sleeping with my then-husband. Plus, I spent almost two years of every-other-weekend visits to monitor Oscar to protect Daniel from being physically abused by him again."

Betty gathered her thoughts. "Your mother abused you from the victim position. *Crystal does her best to blame you for what Bart did to her.* Yet, the moment you knew abuse was at play, you reacted instantly and firmly. There are dad issues throughout your family. Crystal and how her dad abandoned her at age two, and then, he denied she ever existed. Stacy has Tim who may never handle the truth that he is gay and remains an alcoholic. Daniel continues to believe that Oscar won't hit him again. Steve remains troubled by his mother's alcoholism and his father's abandonment. Plus, you have Harry who *only liked you when he was drunk.* And then, along came your dad 27 years after he and his wife committed child abuse on Crystal. I have to say that you have been through *many dark forests* in your lifetime, Debbie."

"Yes, and it's finally time for some happiness in my life."

"You have come a long way. I have seen great change in your anger level and improvement on standing your ground. I want to work on your relationship issues, but that is difficult to do if you don't ever date anyone."

"I don't trust my judgment with men. I attract the sick ones."

She chuckled. "Actually, when you walk into a room full of men, you scan it, find the one with a red light on his forehead and seek him out. That red light means he is the sick one. It is time for you to date a guy you probably would label as *boring.*"

"Yeah, that's probably true. I do like charming men."

"I want you to find a guy to date with no red light who is a bit boring."

I laughed. "I don't like boring."

"I know you don't, but try it to see the difference. I will be on vacation for two weeks. See you in a month."

✳ ✳ ✳

Stacy called me a few days later. "Mom, Rory found out about my porn career today. He gave me an ultimatum. 'Either quit the porn, or I'm going to fire you.'"

"What was your answer?"

"I told him that I like being interviewed, modeling and making porn movies, so I quit my job."

"Honey, can you make enough money in porn to live? I'm sure those movie roles won't come along every day."

"I'm going to buy me a camcorder and set up a nightly show in my apartment."

"What's a camcorder?"

"It's like a small movie camera that hooks up to a computer."

"How can you make money doing that in your apartment?" *Naïve little me thought he meant he'd be dancing.*

"Guys will pay an online fee to see me strip, Mom."

"Oh! Well at least you'll be in your own apartment."

Stacy chuckled. He could tell that I was still struggling with his sudden *porn star outing.*

✳ ✳ ✳

My whole world had just flipped upside down. I didn't know which way to turn. Then, my phone rang. It was George Austin. "How about supper and a drink tomorrow tonight?"

"Make that two drinks, and it's a deal."

When he arrived at my front door the following night, I was still looking for my *Happy Face* and couldn't find it. I opened my door. "I think I need a drink before dinner."

"You look like you could use a shoulder to cry on tonight."

"That's an understatement."

At dinner, we sat there a long time. George wanted to hear why I was so out of sorts. I couldn't tell him, since I didn't know him that well, other than the times I had seen him at a Methodist Singles Group activity. When he drove me home, he came inside and kissed me in the hallway. I had to admit that I was in desperate need of some positive attention, because I was extremely blue.

George hugged me and whispered in my ear. "Let's get married tomorrow and elope to Galveston."

I laughed. "No way. I have enough problems in my life right now without adding anymore."

"I'm serious. I want you to be my wife."

In an *enormous moment of stupidity and weakness,* I agreed. "Okay, but I need four days to get ready."

"I'll make all the arrangements. All I need is you there beside me looking like a *Vision from Heaven.*"

He kissed me, my cheek, my hand, and left.

✻ ✻ ✻

When I woke up the next day, I had a thought. *Surely, that was a bad dream last night. I didn't just agree to elope, did I?*

My phone rang. "Hi doll, I bought our plane tickets, hired a Justice of the Peace in Galveston, and you and I need to go downtown when we arrive to apply for our Marriage License."

"I thought maybe I just dreamed all of that."

"No, you didn't dream it. We're doing it. I'm on my way right now to buy a new suit."

"Boy, you don't let any grass grow under your feet, do you?"

"Nope, when I see something I want, I go for it. See you in three days."

Before George arrived to pick me up, I had an argument with myself. *Are you out of your ever-lovin' mind? How can I explain this to my family and friends? Well, I have been single a long time, and I do get lonely a lot. I've known him several years.* I called Ivan at work and asked for a week's vacation.

The next four days were a blur. I retrieved my gorgeous, white wedding dress with a long train, white hat and a pair of white satin high heels that I had recently paid off in layaway. Plus, George got a surprise. I had my long hair done up in Bo Derrick braids. I took the easy way out and didn't tell anyone what we were doing. Instead, I had some small wedding announcements quickly printed up and mailed them out right before we flew to Galveston. After we landed, I met a couple George had known for a long time. They wanted to be with us at the Galveston Water Gardens when we said "I do." They even agreed to take some pictures of us with my camera.

✳ ✳ ✳

When we flew back home, George stayed at my house for a few nights. His home was over an hour from where I lived. We hung out in my swimming pool for a couple of days, and then I surprised him. "I want you to meet my Psychotherapist, Betty T."

"Psychotherapist? Why do you need one of those?"

"I have quite a few difficult family issues that she's helping me with right now."

"You don't need her, you've got me now."

"Oh, it doesn't work that way. I still need to continue my work with her."

George stood up in a huff. "Then, it's time for me to go home. When are you going to be there?"

"I'll call and let you know. Probably in two days. It's a long drive back-and-forth from your house to my work."

✳ ✳ ✳

The next day, I knew it was time to call Mother first. "Hi, Momma, I know you're wondering about my elopement with George."

"I have to admit, it was quite a shock. When will we meet George?"

"Not right away. I'm about to fly to Toronto, Canada, to attend the National CWA Convention for a week. It will have to be after I get back home."

"Harry and I are eager to meet the man who swept you off your feet so rapidly."

Next, I phoned Crystal. "Hi, honey. We just got back from our honeymoon in Galveston. We had a great time!"

"What possessed you to elope?" Where did you meet this guy, anyway?"

"I met him at the Methodist Singles Group. He seems like a nice guy, and he reminds somewhat of my dad."

"I thought you hated your dad?"

"Hate is a heavy word. Dislike intensely is what I feel."

"Well, I hope you're happy with your new guy who looks like your dad."

Two down, one to go! I phoned Stacy. "Hi sweetie, did you get my wedding notice in the mail?"

"No, I haven't picked up my mail lately. Did you get married?"

"Stupidly, yes, I did. I leave next week for Toronto to attend the CWA Convention."

"I hope things work out for you, Mom!"

"Thanks, honey!"

"Mom, one of my forum fans named Tony980 sent me a few questions for you. Do you have a moment before going out of town to answer them?"

I laughed. "Sure, as long as they aren't too intrusive." Then, I hung up. *At least I have one child who isn't always in my face about something.*

✶ ✶ ✶

Before I went to bed that night, I opened my e-mail and found Tony980's Sawyer Stallion Forum questions for me in my in-box and answered them.

"What writers have influenced you the most?"

"Tennessee Williams and Alexander Poe."

"What quality in Sawyer are you most proud of?"

"His caring nature."

"Which of Sawyer's accomplishments make you most proud of him?"

"That he is still in AA and was such a success in the bar business."

"What new fields of endeavor do you see Sawyer pursuing in say the next five years?"

"My answers are: directing independent films, producing feature films, writing another *Rocky Horror Picture Show* type movie, but one that's his own design and creation of characters which will also live on as a testament to his great talent."

"Any secret *Mom-Type dreams* you have for your son?"

"Yes, I hope to see him own 100% of a successful business which he creates one day. The industry is not important."

"Sawyer seems very focused and driven to achieve his goals. Does he get that from you?"

"Yes, and I believe he will agree with me that he does get that focus from Mom."

"Sawyer says you two wrote two plays together for a ten-minute play competition. How has that turned out?

"Wonderful! I'd like to see them performed live on stage. They are both tremendous!!

Next, Tony980 added this brief note after his list of seven questions for me. "Finally, I'd like to complement you on having such an open, friendly, sincere and gentlemanly son. Thanks, Tony980."

My reply to Tony980's final comment was easy. "Thank *you* for the sincere compliment. Mothers don't often hear such praise about their children."

✳ ✳ ✳

The next day was Saturday. It was time for another Daniel and Oscar four-hour visitation. Steve dropped Daniel off. He came inside with his Gameboy tucked under his arm.

"Hi, do you want to see a movie or play video games today?"

He was evasive and distant. "I don't know." He immediately dove back into his Gameboy.

Oscar phoned me. "I'm parked out front in my truck."

Daniel heard me say, "We're waiting on you. Have you made a decision about what you want to do today?"

He rushed outside to see Oscar, before I could stop him. When he returned, I said, "Daniel, what did you decide?"

"I really don't feel good. I'm upset about what my dad told me today."

"Your dad or Steve?"

"Steve. He told me something that upset me."

"Was that before you got to my house?"

"Yes."

"Is it something I probably know about?"

"Uh-huh. *He told me not to tell anyone.*"

"Oh. I understand." *What is it with Steve always telling me and the kids not to tell anyone what he has said? I don't like it!*

The moment Oscar entered the house, Daniel and I stopped our conversation. As we walked out to Oscar's truck, but were out of his earshot, I whispered to Daniel, "Is this the first time this subject was brought up to you by Steve?"

"Yes."

When Oscar stopped at the video game place, they bought tokens. I phoned Crystal on a payphone. "Crystal, tell me what you and Steve have settled on that you couldn't talk about on the phone to me the other day."

"Why?"

"Is Steve there?"

"No, why?"

"Apparently, Steve had a talk with Daniel about your marriage, right before he dropped him off at my home today. *I think it was bad timing and poorly handled. Especially, after he told Daniel not to tell anyone."*

"Exactly what did he say?"

"I don't know. He didn't get a chance to tell me, but he's quite upset. I'll go get him and you can ask him. Hang on."

I found Daniel on a stool playing Mortal Kombat. "Daniel, your mom wants to talk to you on the phone."

"Where is she?"

"On the payphone in the lobby. Come with me."

Daniel followed me quite reluctantly and took the receiver from me. "Hello, Mom… Yeah, about you not loving him anymore, and you may file for divorce... I'm sad... I want to live with you in my school district. Bye, here's Nana."

"Steve didn't handle this right, Crystal."

"I agree. Today, he moved into his office, and he bought himself a mattress to sleep on. He's now using the kid's bathroom."

"Oh? Do they all know?"

"I explained it as best I could. They think it's neat."

"Why is that?"

"That way, they sleep with Mom. Maybe this will ease them into the divorce idea."

"Maybe, but did Steve tell you that he was going to do this to Daniel today on the way to my house?

"No, I agree it would have been best if we'd done it together."

"True, but he's the adult here, hurt or not. Daniel is an innocent child. Understand, *I don't like him asking Daniel to keep secrets.* Betty will tell you, *'Keeping secrets, keeps people sick.'* "

"Are you sure Steve did this?"

"I understood Daniel to say that is what happened."

She answered with excessive silence.

"How are you doing, Crystal?"

"I'm making it. Daniel seemed to relax, after I assured him we'd stay in his school district. He also said that he wants to live with me, if I move."

"I'm not surprised. I better go. I'll talk to you later. I love you."

"I love you, Mom."

✳ ✳ ✳

I spent the night with George at his ranch home which was in a tiny town with only three thousand people, before I was to fly to Toronto the next day. He cooked us a delicious Italian dish, and then we took a swim in his pool. After that, he poured us some wine and in no time, we were in bed. His lovemaking was overly rough and detached, as if I was merely some remote vessel for his sexual satisfaction. Needless to say, I was turned off by him.

The next morning, he opened his closet door, pulled out a well-worn ladies fur coat and handed it to me. "I want you to wear this. It isn't my size."

"Where did you get it?"

"It belonged to my last wife coat. She died of cancer several years ago. You'll look good in it."

"Why don't you keep it? I'm sure it holds many memories of her for you."

"No, I don't have any."

George's remark hit a nerve with me. *His last wife died of cancer, and he has zero good memories of her?* Because he kept on insisting that I accept her coat, I went ahead and took it. "Are you sure about this?"

"What did I say?"

Not exactly an endearing remark from my new husband. I gathered my things, kissed him, and drove home to get ready to catch my flight to Toronto.

✳ ✳ ✳

I no sooner landed in Toronto and checked in at my hotel, when George phoned to make sure I was there. "I'm driving to Florida to see my mom and sister. Can you change your return flight and fly there instead to meet them?"

"Of course, I can. I would love to meet your family."

"Bye, doll face."

I hung up and shook my head. *You just married a New York Italian. This must be how they all act.*

The whole convention week was a wonderful whirlwind. I was on their Credentials Committee, which meant that I got to sit onstage and listen to all of the speakers, including Hillary Clinton and Richard Gephardt.

✳ ✳ ✳

That evening, I changed my return flight to Miami, FL. When I saw that many attendees had signed up to do a half-day bus ride to see Niagara Falls, I joined them. I had always dreamed of seeing one of the *Seven Wonders of the World* in person. It seemed that every picture I took that day was a keeper.

After doing some souvenir shopping, I joined a group of people and took the boat ride into Niagara Falls. We had to wear yellow plastic slickers to keep from getting drenched.

Our visit ended way too soon. Later, the bus returned us to our Toronto hotel within hours.

✳ ✳ ✳

The next morning, I caught a cab to the Toronto Airport and flew to Miami, Florida. George picked me up in his car and drove us to a Holiday Inn. "My mom and sister are going to meet us in the restaurant in thirty minutes."

"Great, let me change clothes."

Quickly, I pulled out a purple dress from my suitcase and changed in the bathroom. When I walked out, George looked me over. "Yeah, you'll do."

I had no answer for that remark, so I managed a weak smile. He escorted me to the Holiday Inn Restaurant. His mother and sister were already there. George introduced us. "Mom, Sis, this is my new wife, Debbie."

They each nodded at me and mumbled something.

I smiled. "It's so nice to meet both of you."

We ordered our food. While we waited on it, George and his family got into a fight over a family matter. Much of their conversation was in Italian, so I was totally in the dark. When our food arrived, everyone ate their food without saying a word, so I decided to break the ice. "What a great meal this was. Seafood in Florida is the best."

The three of them ignored me and resumed their angry discussion in Italian. The next thing I knew, George jumped up and fled the restaurant. I felt I needed to follow him outside. "Is there any way to calm this disagreement down, so you can enjoy being with your family?"

Apparently, that was the wrong thing to say. He stormed off and left me standing there all alone. Rather than follow him back inside, I went to our room to change clothes and watch TV. He showed up an hour later, didn't speak, took a shower and went to sleep.

The next morning, George dressed very early. "I'll be out front with the car."

I took a shower, dressed and took my suitcase out front to George's car. During our three day drive home, he barely uttered twelve words to me the whole trip. *Halfway home, I wanted out of our marriage and fast! Dark moods do not work for me and never will.*

18

≈

Where There's a Will, I'll Find a Way

After George dropped me off at my home, he took my suitcase out of his car trunk, kissed me on the cheek and drove away without saying a word. *That did it! I'm done with George.*

Once inside my home, I left my suitcase in the foyer hall and sat down on the couch. *What a horrible trip with my so-called husband! I just had to pick another sick man.*

I stood up to get a soda pop, noticed my message light was on and listened to my messages. The first three calls were from Steve. "Debbie, call me." "Where are you, Debbie?" "I need to talk to you! Please call me!"

The last message was from Stacy. "Mom, a strange thing has happened. I want to tell you about it. Call me ASAP!"

They all sounded urgent, but I called Stacy first. "Hi, honey, I just walked in and got your message. What's up?"

"While you were gone, I had three dreams about you. They all told me the same thing to tell you. Can I come over? I want to tell you in person."

"Okay, I just got home. I'll be here."

✳ ✳ ✳

Stacy arrived in twenty minutes and came in with his key. He hurried into the den with an air of excitement and sat close to me.

"Seriously, I had this same exact dream about you three nights in a row while you were gone."

"Okay, tell me about it."

"Each dream told me that *you must write a book.*"

I was stunned. "That's amazing!"

"Yes, and there's more. In each dream, the next scene showed me sitting in a room of important people at a long table. There was one empty seat at the head of the table. Everyone was eagerly awaiting your arrival. When you came in, you were still beautiful, but obviously older. You were famous for your book."

That moment took me back quite a few years to June 23, 1985, when I first met Bertie Catchings. It was now September 17, 1992. For a few minutes, I was speechless. Finally, I stood up. "Let me show you something." I walked to my formal living room, opened a desk drawer and pulled out the same yellow legal pad I took with me when I first saw Bertie Catchings. I was so excited about Stacy's dreams, I totally forgot about Steve's messages. I showed him a few pages on my yellow legal pad that I wrote after my first reading with Bertie.

"Honey, this is where I actually attempted to begin writing a book about what Bart did. I titled it *Snake Charmer.* I wrote about three pages, but my pain was still too fresh from that awful morning when I found that white satchel in his Blazer. I had to stop. I tossed the pad in that desk drawer and hadn't looked at it again until today. I guess Bertie was right after all. *I am supposed to write a book.*"

"You never mentioned it to me, Mom."

"That's because of my pain and depression. Let's go have lunch and write an outline for the book to help me try again."

Stacy drove us to Denny's. We had breakfast, and soon developed a two-page outline that we both liked. I laughed, "I guess it's time to kick start my book again."

Later, he dropped me off at home. I hurried inside, eager to start writing as soon as possible. Instead, my phone was ringing. I knew it must be Steve. I had forgotten all about his messages. Hurriedly, I picked up the receiver. "Steve, what's going on?"

Before he spoke, I could hear my grandkids weeping in the background. All I could think was, *"Oh my God, Crystal's dead!"*

Steve's voice was hoarse. "This time, she insists she's gone for good and never coming back. She left all four kids here with me. She's already rented an apartment across town."

"Oh, that's just great! She thinks she's done being a Mom to her kids? It doesn't work that way. Kids are a lifetime decision. Mom's don't divorce their kids."

I could hear the finality in Steve's voice. "I'm just going to move on with my life and take care of these kids."

"I can tell you that Oscar will go to court and take Daniel away from you, if he can. I have plenty of documentation from my Supervised Visitation to help show that he is still an unfit parent."

"Let's cross that bridge when we come to it."

"Give me Crystal's apartment address before you hang up." Steve quickly rattled off her phone number and address. I jotted both of them on my yellow legal pad. *Not exactly how I had planned to start my book.*

"Steve, I'm here for you and the kids. Let me know anytime I can help you or them. And I want to apologize for Crystal's behavior."

"Thanks, that means a lot, but I can't hold you responsible for her behavior."

"I know, but *I feel so helpless and embarrassed that my daughter would do this to her own children.*"

✷ ✷ ✷

The following night, George phoned me. "Honey, I'm sorry I was such a grouch. Can we forget about what happened and move on?"

"Actually, I can't recall what happened. Remind me."

"You know I'm Italian. We aren't the best at relationships, sometimes. We argue, wave our hands and rage occasionally."

"Well, I wasn't raised that way. I don't handle screaming."

"Come on, give me another chance. I'd like to meet your parents."

"Okay, we can drive there this weekend to see them. Let me check with them first."

"Great! You know I love you."

"Do I? You have a funny way of showing it."

"I messed up. Let me make it up to you."

"I'll call Mother and see what she says."

The following morning, I phoned Mother. "Hi, Momma, George would like for us to drive up there this Saturday. He wants to meet you and Harry."

"We'll be here, honey."

On Saturday, George showed up all smiles and drove us to Mother's house. We had a nice visit. She seemed impressed with him. Probably because he looked so much like my dad. George smirked, after we left. "I told you I could be a nice guy. I could tell they liked me."

"Yes, they seemed to like you."

He stopped in front of my home. "Why don't you come to my house for the weekend?"

"I would, except there's a problem with Crystal that I need to take care of tomorrow. I'll drive to your place, after I get off work Monday night and spend the night."

He took my hand. "Why don't you sell your home and just move in with me?"

"No, I like my home. I don't want to sell it."

He grinned, "See you Monday evening, my love."

When I stepped out of his car, I felt like I had just dealt with a *Used Car Salesman*. I wasn't the least bit impressed.

✳ ✳ ✳

On Sunday, I phoned Crystal. "Hi, I'd like to come over today and see you, unless you're busy."

"What makes you think I'm busy?"

"Just checking, honey. Don't want to interrupt anything."

An hour later, I knocked on Crystal's apartment door. When she let me in, I was surprised to see all new furniture. "Looks like you've been shopping."

"I had no choice. I needed furniture."

My quick scan around the small room bothered me. "Where are you going to put your kids?"

"I gave them to Steve. I'm not able to handle the kids right now."

"Why not?"

"I'm in a bad place. *I need time to be me for a while.*"

"And you don't think your children need you?"

"You know what? I don't want to hear it. Don't lecture me."

"I'm not lecturing. I'm concerned about my grandchildren. They need to be with their mother."

"Well, it's time for me to take care of me for a while and no one else."

"Maybe you should have thought about that before you had four children?"

"I'm not going back to him. I can't deal with them right now. They're better off with Steve."

"You know that I love you, Crystal, but I don't like your decision one little bit."

"I didn't ask you to, Mom. It's my life, not yours."

"Okay, but I could hear those sweet kids weeping yesterday in the background, when Steve called me. It broke my heart."

Crystal screwed up her mouth, just like Mother would do when she knows she's done something to me she shouldn't have done. I just shook my head and left.

✱ ✱ ✱

My routine at work changed drastically because of the recent call Johnny had received from his boss. Instead of having lunch once in a while at the same table with Johnny and several of my co-workers, I decided to sit at a table-for-two against the wall as my private lunch spot. Each afternoon, I wrote on my book and took an occasional bite of lunch. My co-workers were all dying of curiosity. One-by-one, they quizzed me about what I was writing. *Frankly, it is none of their business, just like it is not their business if Johnny and I are friends.* My standing answer became, "It's a book about people who've been abused."

One day, Johnny overheard my reply to one of the biggest busybodies, Ruby Hart, and winked at me as he left the room. Ruby didn't earn her company position on ability. Instead, when I was handling the case for *Spare Wheel*, she played a huge part in trying to cost him his job permanently.

The minute I discovered that my *sometime friend* had intentionally sold out Spare Wheel to gain a company position; I would have nothing to do with her, unless I had to work in her area. She spent many months trying to get back in my good graces. When she realized that she was wasting her time, she began to harass me anytime I worked in her area.

✱ ✱ ✱

Two weeks later, I agreed to try and spend at least three nights a week at George's home. My concern remained the long drive to his home, to work and then to his place at nighttime after work.

I will never forget the first Thursday night I drove to his home one night. I parked beside his car, used my door key and entered his large, rambling ranch house. No lights were on anywhere, so I flipped on the hallway light. "George, are you here?" No reply. At first, I felt sure he must be there somewhere, since his car was out front. Again, I called out. "George?" No response.

Slowly, I turned the corner into his long den. I could see a shadow in the middle of the dark room sitting in a chair. I inched toward the shadow and discovered *it was George sitting in the dark.*

"George, you scared me. What's the matter?" *Someone in his family must have passed away or something.* I waited for the longest time, but he didn't move or say a word. *This must be what a Black Mood looks like.* Finally, I turned to leave.

"Where do you think you're going?"

"Home! I don't know what's going on with you, but I don't like it."

Suddenly, he darted toward me and grabbed me with his strong hands. "You aren't going anywhere."

"Let go of me!"

"You're my wife."

"This isn't how a wife is supposed to be treated."

He shifted gears and became the same guy I thought I had married. "I bought you something special."

"Okay?"

He led me into his kitchen. On the table, I saw a small box. I opened it to find some long, diamond-shaped, silver earrings. "Do you like them?"

"Yes, they're very nice."

That night, I couldn't sleep much. I tossed-and-turned for fear that George may do something else bizarre. *Why do I attract such sick men?*

I got up early, put a note on the table and left. The note read: *"George, I have an appointment this morning."*

✳ ✳ ✳

Once at home, I changed clothes and relaxed before I left to see Betty before work. At first, I hesitated to tell her about my marriage, so I told her about Stacy's new career and updated her on all of the other family issues that had happened during the time she was gone on vacation.

"I'm quite pleased with the way you handled getting the news about Stacy's porn career. Now, I want to talk about how lonely you have been all of your life. Who did you talk to?"

I looked at my lap. "Smokey Joe, my Cocker Spaniel. He was all I had." Finally, I found my courage. "Betty, I eloped with George Austin while you were gone."

She stared at me in disbelief and then laughed. "Well, I can see that we still have a whole lot of work to do yet."

"I know. I can't believe I did that to myself. It was in a bad moment, and he showed up. You're not mad at me, are you?"

"No, I'm not, but are you mad at yourself?"

"Yes, but I can't unring a bell. At least, my last name is still Austin."

"Tell me all about George and your new life with him."

I spent the next thirty minutes relating the good, bad and the totally unacceptable behavior I saw in George.

"Do you realize how controlling this man is to you?"

"Without question, yes I do!"

"What do you plan to do about him?"

"I won't live with yet another out-of-control man. What if I ask him to come see you?"

"That's a start, but his first visit must be with both of you."

"I'll talk to him about it tonight, when I drive to his home after I get off work."

Betty changed the subject. "Your mother and Harry always felt sorry for Crystal, because she didn't have any family except Tim's family."

I stared at her. "Then, who felt sorry for me?"

"You tell me."

"All I can think of is Granny, Pop Sherman and Smokey Joe."

"And how does that make you feel?"

"Like an orphan."

"Let's talk about the girl at your work named Lori. Do you consider her a friend?"

"Yes, most of the time."

"When haven't you considered her a friend?"

"The day she challenged me about seeing you."

"Are there any more times you can think of?"

"Yes, all of the times when she would call me at home to dump her troubles in my lap for hours, but the moment I brought up one of my problems, she had to go."

"Do you not see how abusive she is to you?"

"I guess. She also makes plans with me to go somewhere, but so many times she'll call me at the last minute to tell me that something else popped up she wants to do it instead."

"What kind of things were they?"

"Her family would drop by unannounced fifteen minutes before she was to leave, or a friend just came to town without notice."

"Weren't you hurt by that?"

"Sure, because it happened so many times."

"Lori is a very abusive friend. It is time for you to pull away from her. Don't be her Surrogate Sponsor anymore."

✳ ✳ ✳

I used Betty's lobby phone to call Stacy. "Hi, how about having lunch with me, before I drive to work today?"

"Sure! Call me when you get here."

"Will do." I hung up and went to my car in the parking area. I soon knocked on Stacy's door. He came outside.

"Let's go. I have some good news to tell you on the way."

"Wonderful! Good news is what I need to hear right now."

As I drove down the street, Stacy pointed. "Turn right at the next corner."

"Where are we going?"

"It's a surprise. In four blocks, turn left into a small shopping center."

When I did, I stopped my car. "Now what?"

He pointed at a vacant building in the center of the shopping center. "One day soon, that will be a brand new gay bar, and I will be a co-owner."

"How is that going to happen?"

"One of Rory's competitors approached me about being a co-owner of a new gay bar. His money, my skills, and I run it."

"That's amazing! I'm happy for you, honey. What are you going to name it?"

"The Out-Look Club."

"That's a clever name for a gay bar. I like it."

✳ ✳ ✳

Thankfully, work was uneventful that night. While I ate my supper at the small table and worked on my book, I noticed someone had left a Junior College flyer for upcoming classes across town. I opened the flyer and saw that a Dr. C. Warner was holding a novel writing class twice a week. I stuffed the flyer into my purse.

I was a little blue when I left work that night. My new husband was quickly becoming a huge disappointment, and I missed my friendship with Johnny at work.

When I entered George's front door, he was in the kitchen wearing an apron and cooking supper. Suddenly, he was Mr. Happy. *Why can't I have Mr. Happy twenty-four/seven?*

He was singing an Italian song and cooking supper like a TV chef. The meal he prepared was astoundingly great! Afterward, we shared some wine, and then our lovemaking was remarkably good.

Before we went to sleep, we talked. "I had an interesting visit with Betty today. She thinks it would be helpful if we both visit her together sometime. What do you think?"

Surprisingly, George smiled. "If that will make my baby happy, we'll do it."

He quickly fell asleep. *Why was that so easy?*

✳ ✳ ✳

A week later, Stacy phoned me at home. "Mom, I need to tell you something before you find out from someone else."

"What's that?"

"I got arrested last night."

"What were you doing?"

"I was dancing at a club in Mississippi."

"What were you doing that got you arrested?"

"They hired me to strip. Apparently, they don't allow strippers to remove all of their clothes while performing there."

"I thought you were going to be a co-owner in a new club?"

"The money was too good to pass up, so I took the gig."

"Is this the first time you've done that?"

"No, I had to make a living after Rory let me go. I've done quite a few of these gigs."

"Will your arrest make the TV or the newspaper?"

"I don't know."

It feels like Pandora's Box just knocked the breath out of me! I'm at a loss for words. Visions of my son locked up in a Mississippi jail cell haunted me for weeks.

✳ ✳ ✳

19

≈

Love Your Children, Even Though

After Stacy's phone call, I gave my latest dilemma a lot of soul searching. For years, I fought through *Hell and High Water* to save my son from the clutches of drugs and alcoholism; I stood firm as I fought two doctors from erroneously declaring him crazy and locking him up in an insane asylum, after an AA member intentionally tried to destroy his mind with a dangerous drug that left him looking and acting like a hopeless vegetable. I learned to accept the fact that he had always been gay and that no church program or person could ever change that fact.

Am I now going to turn my back on him because of his new life as a Porn Star? In today's world, there are millions of people who watch porn on a daily basis, mostly done in secret. I know that the stigma of being a Porn Star will forever remain part of his resume. Where is it written that a mother must stop loving her son, because he's involved in the porn industry?

I turned to my King James Bible for an answer. "Therefore judge nothing before the time, until the Lord come, who will bring to light the hidden things of darkness and will make manifest the counsels of the hearts, and then shall *every man have praise of God.* 1 Corinthians 4: 5."

From that moment forward, I decided to stand by my son and continue to love and support him, knowing full well that I may experience a myriad of naysayers and haters. *There will also be those mothers who have walked in my shoes beside their gay children and chose love instead of excommunication and acceptance in the place of disdain.* My new mantra quickly became, "I love my children, even though I do not always like their decisions or behavior."

✳ ✳ ✳

It was during this new mindset that I picked up my phone and called Mother. "I want to know why you have never liked Stacy. Even when he was two-years-old, I knew you didn't like him, and I couldn't understand it. How can anyone not like a young child?"

Mother played innocent. "I don't know what you're talking about."

"Yes, you do. Yesterday, your longtime friend, Mary, called me. She commented on how you never liked Stacy, and you even talked about it to her. Why is that, Mother?"

"I guess it was the time they were here as youngsters for the weekend. Crystal got into the bathtub. Without me knowing it, Stacy pulled off his clothes and jumped in the tub with her. I never could get over it."

"What was there to get over? He was only three at the time. Apparently, you didn't realize that I usually bathed them together when they were that young. Since then, he has always felt you never liked or loved him. I find that fact to be extremely sad."

"You know, I'd like Granny's furniture back if you ever move out of your home." *What did my mother just say? How typical of her to change the subject whenever I confront her. It's her same old sick stuff. She gives me things, and then, she wants them back.*

✳ ✳ ✳

On Monday, I woke up determined to make some more changes in my life. I phoned the Eastern Junior College and enrolled in Dr. Warner's novel writing class on Tuesday and Thursday nights for six weeks.

When I arrived at work, Lori immediately approached me. "Debbie, how about we go to a movie this Saturday?"

I smiled. "Thanks, but George and I may have plans."

She looked a bit miffed. "Oh, I forgot about him."

"Sure you did." I left her standing there and went to talk with Jackie and Karla.

After work, I phoned George. "Hi, I spoke with Betty. She has us scheduled to meet with her in two weeks."

"Great to hear that, baby. You know, I've been thinking about things. Why not sell your house and move in with me, then you can cash in your profit sharing, and I'll take real good care of you."

"That isn't something I want to do right now. Why don't you come over here and stay with me this weekend? We can see a movie or go dancing."

"Sure thing. I love spending time with my beautiful doll."

✳ ✳ ✳

During the next two weeks at work, I tried to keep my distance from Lori. Occasionally, I went out to lunch with Jackie or Karla. At least, I didn't feel like they were using me as a dumping ground for their personal problems. It was rather refreshing.

I also began to attend my novel writing classes with Dr. Warner. One evening after my fourth class, he approached me. "Debbie, I am quite impressed with your writing. I believe you have some real writing talent. Would you consider letting me work with you on your novel?"

"Are you serious?"

"Yes, I am. I'd like to become your *Hip Pocket Agent*."

"What does that mean?"

"When you have at least six polished chapters, I will submit them to a publisher."

"What will it cost me?"

"Nothing, until a publisher wants your book, then I get a percentage."

I grinned. "Of course, I'll work with you on it."

✳ ✳ ✳

The next day, I kept my appointment with Betty at nine a.m. and brought up my book. "Would you write an epilogue and a preface for my book?"

Unexpectedly, she began to ask me pointed questions. "Why did you stay with Bart so long?"

"Because I loved him, and he treated me like a queen."

"What did you get from him that kept you there?"

"I thought he walked on water and was basically a good husband and father."

"Didn't you ever fight?"

"It happened only three or four times in eleven years."

"Don't you realize he exploited your values and controlled and abused you?"

"I never felt controlled. Bart got his way with charm. He was my protector when I needed him to be."

"Did he ever make advances toward Stacy?"

"Not that I know of, but when Stacy wrote that letter to Pia Mellody and asked if *sexual abuse could cause him to be gay* it certainly made me wonder about it."

"How do you feel now that Crystal is coming to therapy?"

"It makes me happy."

Betty's accidental comment, after that, totally shocked me.

"Daniel is coming with Crystal tomorrow for her visit."

"Really? I didn't know that."

"I made a slip. I shouldn't have said that. How do you feel about Daniel?"

"He's so special. He's a precious little boy with gorgeous eyes, and he's a computer whiz. His dad is in Court Ordered Therapy. Daniel learned an important lesson this past week. He lied to his school teachers about why he forgot his homework. Then, he told another lie to cover up another lie, and he got caught. Crystal asked Steve to agree to ground him for three weeks. When I heard about it, I phoned Daniel, 'Your mom loves you enough to teach you the value of telling the truth. One day, you will thank her.' "

"Betty, I also confronted Mother about how she has treated Stacy for so many years."

"Let me guess. She was evasive, wounded and then pointed you in another direction to avoid the truth about Stacy." I nodded.

✶✶✶

Steve's attorney phoned me the next day. "Debbie, I need for you to type up your visitation notes on Oscar and e-mail them to me before next Monday. He is trying to force Steve to give him full custody of Daniel."

"No problem. It will be a lot of typing, but I'm pretty fast at the keyboard. You'll have them tomorrow."

"Great! Can you meet us at the courthouse with Daniel on Tuesday, in case Judge Groff wants to talk to either one of you?"

"Definitely, we can be there. What about Steve and Crystal? Will they be there, too?"

"Yes, inside the Judge Groff's Courtroom, but you and Daniel can wait outside in the hallway."

I hung up. *I guess Steve and Crystal haven't told his attorney they are separated yet.*

I spent all day Saturday typing up my copious visitation notes for Steve's attorney, and then, I e-mailed them to him.

✳ ✳ ✳

George was waiting in the parking lot when I got off work Monday night. I slid inside his car, and he smiled. "What sounds good to eat, doll?"

"You know me. I love good seafood."

He drove us to the nearest Red Lobster. We went inside and ordered. "How did your business meeting go at the bank today?"

"I had to straighten out all of my bank accounts."

"How many do you have?"

"Four right now."

"Why so many?"

"I have one for my anvils, one for my school where I teach horseshoeing, one for my farrier business and a personal one."

"Why not combine some of them?"

He leaned close and whispered. "Look, I don't pay Uncle Sam his fair share of taxes. I move my money in-and-out of accounts to make it harder for the IRS to figure out what I owe them each year in taxes."

"Isn't that illegal?"

"Only if I get caught."

As he drove me to my house to spend the night together, my mind was in a whirlwind. *I can't be married to someone who's cheating the government, and I darn sure won't file any tax returns with him.*

✳ ✳ ✳

I phoned Betty the next day from work. "Betty, do you have any openings this week? I feel it's important for George and me to meet with you right away."

"As a matter of fact, someone had to cancel their appointment for Thursday at ten a.m."

"We'll be there."

On Thursday, I introduced George to Betty, and we sat down. She asked him some personal questions about his family. "Are you and your family close? How do you approach problems with others? What do you hope to accomplish from today's meeting?"

He seemed overly defensive. "Italian families are always close. I handle problems fairly good. I want Debbie and me to be happy together."

Betty smiled. "Those are all good answers. Here is what I want you and Debbie to do. I am going to give each of you a list of things for you to work on in your relationship. On our next visit, we will discuss how things have gone since today." Betty wrote out two short lists and handed one to each of us.

He studied his list and smiled. "It's a piece of cake."

Then, he drove me to work. "I have a business meeting this afternoon at my bank. I'll pick you up when you get off." He kissed me and drove away.

✳ ✳ ✳

That night, we stayed at my home and read our lists from Betty to each other before we went to bed. When I turned out the light, George fell fast asleep in seconds. The next morning, he arose like he'd been shot. I quickly rallied. "What's wrong?"

He shouted. "I can't do it! *I can never do it!*"

I sat up in the bed. "You can't do what?"

"That list of things from Betty; I can't do any of them."

I climbed out of bed and looked him in the eye. "Then, I won't stay married to you. I'm going to file for divorce."

"And who's going to pay for that?"

"We can split the filing fee. I will be my own attorney and draw up an agreement for us to sign."

"Return the diamond wedding band I bought you."

"Only if you give me the diamond wedding band I gave you."

"Give me my fur coat back."

"Gladly, it never felt right for me to have it." I opened my closet, grabbed the faded fur and tossed it at him."

As he left, relief swept through me like a welcome breeze. I walked to the den, and Crystal phoned. "Mom, I need a favor. Would you write me a professional resume, so I can get a job?"

"Of course, I will. Get me a list of your references, what type of position you want and any experience you have."

"Okay, I will e-mail you a short resume in a few minutes."

"By the way, I'm divorcing George."

"I'm not surprised. It happened way too fast."

"Tell me!" I hung up and quickly created a professional resume, after she sent me the requested info.

✳ ✳ ✳

Later that day, I drove to work without my wedding ring. *It felt as if I had just escaped from prison.* When I walked in the side door at work, the Union Secretary cornered me in the lunchroom and whispered, "Lori has filed charges against you."

I laughed. "What kind of charges?"

"She claims that you won't speak to her anymore, and since you are our Union President, she has requested that *the Union must force you be her friend and speak to her again.*"

I couldn't stop laughing. "There is no law that says I have to speak to anyone, and there certainly is no law that says the Union can force me to be her friend. *My job is to represent people, not be abused by them.*"

She began to sputter. "She has rights, too."

"Forget it. Go take it up with an Investigation Committee. They will tell you the same thing that I just told you."

I left her standing there all aghast and went to work as if nothing had happened. Ivan put me into Ruby Hart's department for the whole week, so I knew something was up.

✳ ✳ ✳

Sure enough, two days later, Ruby went to Ivan's office with some work that I turned in to her. I watched her continually point in my direction. Then, she scurried to her desk and began to search through her desk drawers. My work area faced away from her desk. Suddenly, she threw a handful of something metal into her trash can and stated loud enough for me to hear, "If anyone gets into my trash can again, they better be careful. I just put Exacto razor blades in it." I had my gut full of Ruby Hart's meanness and lies. The next day, I wisely made copies of every piece of work I turned in to her that day. I also put a voice activated tape recorder inside my slightly open desk drawer.

In no time, Ruby issued a loud threat to me, so the other two women working near me could hear it. "Debbie, I know you are trying to make me look bad to Ivan. I won't stand for it."

"What are you talking about?"

"You know exactly what I'm talking about. I'm marking up the ads correctly, and you are doing every one of them wrong on purpose. You're making me look bad, because the ads are late."

"Not one word you just spoke to me is true."

She began to shake. "Are you calling me a liar?"

"I merely stated that your claim is not true."

"See, you just called me a liar again. I'll get you fired for that. It's insubordination!"

Ruby jumped to her feet, grabbed papers from her desk and stormed into Ivan's office. I watched her hands waving and pointing at me for over ten minutes. Finally, she strutted back to her chair, plopped down and gave me a hateful glare. Ivan came over two minutes later. "Debbie, I need to see you in my office."

"Sure. I'll be right there." I picked up my copies of the ads I did that day along with my tape recorder and went into Ivan's office. I listened to him repeat Ruby's false claims about my work that day. Then, I handed him my copies of the ads I had set. "Ivan that is how I produced those ads. Obviously, Ruby changed my work in an effort to get me fired."

He appeared offended. "You can't mean that!"

"Yes, I do. She threatened to get me fired today. And yesterday, she told me in front of my co-workers that she was now throwing razor blades into her trash can, so that *someone*, implying me, would get hurt. That's criminal intent to harm an employee and totally unacceptable."

He blurted out. *"You can't prove any of that."*

I placed my small recorder on his desk and played back Ruby's second theat. He turned pale. "Go back to work."

I nodded, picked up my recorder and left his office.

Ivan summoned Ruby to his office. Apparently, he wasn't too happy that her attempt to get me fired had failed. *Being Union President sure does has its negative points.* I smiled to myself and resumed my work. Their little scheme had failed miserably.

✳ ✳ ✳

On Sunday, I decided it was high time for me to relax and spend some time in my swimming pool. I felt like I had earned it. I put my telephone on a long phone cord and sat it on the back steps inside my screened in porch. I put an Elvis record on my turntable, so I could hear it from my back porch speakers. *It felt like heaven to hop into my pool, float on my raft, enjoy an Elvis serenade and drift off to sleep in the warm sunshine.*

And hour later, my back porch phone rang and woke me up. I slid off my raft and hurried to my phone.

"Did I catch you at a bad time?"

"No, you didn't. Is this Danny S.?"

"Yeah. Have you seen Stacy's big interview yet?"

"No, who is it with?"

"A staff writer named Gene L. with *Fantasy Showcase Magazine.*"

"Never heard of it. How can I find it, so I can read it?"

"Do an online search for *Sawyer Stallion's Interview.*"

"Thanks, I'll do that."

I grabbed my beach towel, dried off and went inside to search the internet for Stacy's *Sawyer Stallion Interview.*" It popped right up and surprised me that it was four pages long. I printed it out, when my phone began to ring off the hook. Various friends of Stacy's called to tell me about his big interview news. *After a little self-talk, I decided to read Sawyer Stallion's Interview.*

20

≈

Interview of a Porn Star

I sat on my couch and read my copy of Stacy's first interview. Honestly, I felt a bit anxious about it, after all, I am Mom...

✳ ✳ ✳

"Given the prominence of straight guys in gay porn, it is understandable that when we first saw big butch Sawyer Stallion in *Cousin Jody*, we thought, ho-hum, he's just another straight top. But when it came time for the sex, we quickly began to notice things. For his first movie, he was fearless and even pinched his own nipples. Not too many straight males do that, but most revealing of all, there was no attitude!"

Gene L.: "Sawyer, what convinced you to take the plunge into XXX videos?"

Sawyer Stallion: "When I did a photo shoot for a local bar magazine, I was pretty comfortable modeling. In truth, I began undressing more than I was supposed to, so the photographer shot a lot of film. His flash kept going and going. Some guys saw the photos and told me that I should consider a career in video. At first, I was against it, but they kept on saying that they thought I'd be a natural, and I started to think. *Well...*"

GL: "When was this?"

SS: "About a year ago. The more they talked about it, the better it sounded. Yet, I thought I needed to do even more nude modeling to build my portfolio first. I did four more sessions with different photographers."

GL: "So, suddenly, you were *out there.*"

SS: "Yeah, probably."

GL: "How did you get from photos to your first video with Bunker Studios?"

SS: "Everyone kept saying, 'Eagleton, Eagleton, that's where you belong.' So I sent my stuff to Eagleton, but never received a return call. I even faxed photos to them twice, and there was no response. Next, I decided to find the best agent in the business."

GL: "There are over sixty of them in our magazine."

SS: "Right. I asked around. One of my friends gave me the name of one of the biggest porn agents in L.A., Nathan K. I called and told him that I wanted to send him some stuff. The day he got my pictures, he faxed me a contract, so I figured he liked what he saw."

"A month later, Nathan got a desperate call. The lead for Rave Studio's upcoming video, *Cousin Jody*, backed out. They needed a replacement and fast. Nathan's assistant rushed their entire book of models, two big volumes, to Rave. Carlos Montez literally flipped through the pages non-stop and suddenly froze. '*Him. I want him!*' So, it was like fate, and that's how I got into the business. I give full credit to my agent."

GL: "Did you have sex with any of the porn stars that performed at the club you managed?"

SS: "No, I discovered that most of them were straight and had sex with our female secretary." (Sawyer laughed.)

GL: "Is making a movie easier or harder than you thought?"

SS: "It was a lot harder than I thought it would be. I had greater, much greater, respect for everybody in the business after doing my first one. *Erection-on-cue is not what you're used to.* It's much different than you can imagine. When I walked onto my first porn set, it was a beautiful set."

GL: "Are you versatile in your personal life, or do you only top?"

SS: "I'm not a virgin. I do prefer a dominant role. I think it's more erotic."

GL: "You're quite a good actor, very natural. Do you have a background in acting?"

SS: "Oh, you know, Drama Club in high school."

GL: "Back then, did you want to move to Hollywood and become a star?"

SS: "No, no. When I was a teenager, I worked for a producer and got to meet famous people like Ruth Warrick and Bob Hope. Ruth was doing a college tour, and I traveled with her and worked backstage, because I worked for the producer."

GL: "And what happened the second time you came to Hollywood to make a video?"

SS: "I had a little behind-the-scenes romance. Is that what you're looking for, some dirt on me?" (Sawyer laughed.)

GL: "Of course! Though *dirt* is not a word I use about this profession. Insight is what I'm after. Is dominance something that you try to project in other relationships as well?"

SS: "I'm not currently in a relationship."

GL: "Would you recommend getting into videos to someone casting about for something to do?"

SS: "You have to want to do it for yourself. You can't do it to prove anything. People ask me why I do videos. My answer; because it is fun, and I had the opportunity, so I took it. It isn't something you are going to make a million dollars doing. It's looked down upon by many people."

GL: "Okay, we know you're gay. Are you are out to your family?"

SS: "Yes."

GL: "Tell all."

SS: "I came out when I was nineteen. It was kind of dramatic. I was still living at home. I was caught naked in our pool with two straight boys. I was trying to seduce them, so I had them naked. We were wrestling. You can see we were going in the right direction, until my mother woke up. We had made too much noise. She flips on the pool light and here are these boys all naked."

"She shouted, 'What are you doing in the pool nude at four in the morning with two other boys? Are you all having sex?' I was extra drunk and had used tequila to get them naked. In answer to her question about having sex, I declared, 'Not yet.' "

"Those boys looked at me and go, 'What?' I was honestly more pissed that she had interrupted us than that we got caught, because I had the hots for one of them real bad."

"The two boys both yelled, 'We're not gay, he is!' "

"Mom insisted, 'So, what are you doing in the pool with my son?' It could almost be a *YMCA* film."

GL: "It sounds like it." (I chuckled.)

SS: "So, it was a little traumatic, but she got over it. When she found out recently that I was doing gay porn, she commented, 'There's nothing you can do now that's going to shock me.' "

GL: "Well, after that pool scene..."

SS: "No, she's way over the gay thing a long time ago. In fact, I'm the centerfold in a new *Cousin Jody* spread. I have it on my coffee table. I know she'll probably pick it up and see it sooner or later, the next time she visits me. If I tried to stop her, I'm kind of sure she'd say, 'You know I've seen it. I've changed your diapers.' She's very supportive."

GL: "So you'd had sex with girls before, just not guys?"

SS: "Yeah, I mean, I always knew I was gay. When you live in *The South*, you get all of this guilt. That's why the Internet is so popular. Guilt can traumatize you."

GL: "What do you see for yourself over the next few years?"

SS: "I'm going to stay in adult video. I hope Rave Studios signs me for another year. I like working with Carlos Montez. I want *Sawyer Stallion* to be a big name. I hope that I can be a big enough name to stay in the business for four or five years. It's kind of a roll of the dice. I don't know what makes somebody a *big name*, but I'd like for there to be at least one gay one. Right?"

And knowing my son, he definitely wants to be that One Big Name Gay someday…

21

≈

Own Your Own Reality

Monday morning rolled around rather rapidly. Steve let me know that he would bring Daniel to court. Crystal called and told me she'd meet me in the hall outside Judge Groff's Courtroom.

When I stepped off the elevator, I could see Crystal sitting on a bench, but no Daniel. "Hi honey, where's Daniel?"

"Steve took him to the restroom. He got gum on his pants."

"I brought some colored pens and paper for Daniel. I thought he might like to draw some pictures, while we sit out here and wait. Any idea if he or I will be needed in the courtroom yet?"

"I haven't heard a word about anything."

Daniel and Steve approached us. "Nana, I got a new haircut." His long hair was gone and replaced by a buzz cut.

The courtroom door flew open. Steve's attorney motioned. "Steve, Crystal, I need you inside now."

I questioned, "Where's Oscar?"

The attorney smiled. "No one has seen him? If he's a no-show, too bad." Crystal and Steve followed the attorney inside.

"Daniel, come sit beside me. I brought some paper, so you can draw pictures today."

He slid onto the bench. "Where's that paper, Nana?"

I opened my purse and handed him a notepad and a box of Crayolas. "Nana, I think I want to draw my dad." He took a red Crayola and began to draw a side view of Oscar.

About that time, Oscar scurried around the corner toward us. He was wearing a tan suit, gray tie and an orange shirt. He stopped in front of me. "Is this the Judge Groff Courtroom?"

"It is right in front of us, yes."

"Have they started yet?"

"About ten minutes ago."

Oscar looked at Daniel's new haircut. "You look like you're ready for the military, son." He turned and flung the big door open and rushed inside.

Daniel continued to draw his picture of Oscar. It proved to be quite interesting, as it took shape. For a ten-year-old, Daniel's art was quite detailed. He drew Oscar's head with huge bug-eyes, shaggy hair in the back and a roundish flattop hat. Scores of lines and circles were shooting out of the hat. From the back of the hat, he drew a big thought cloud. Inside the thought balloon, he drew a picture of Oscar soaking in a tub of water. Oddly, he showed him wearing the same hat with the same set of lines shooting from the hat. *Maybe anger?*

Next, Daniel crayoned a top shirt on Oscar which looked more like a dress, with designs all over it. He drew one of his arms down to his side and added legs. Strangely, there were no feet or shoes, only lots of horizontal scratch-like marks.

He then added three small comment bubbles around Oscar's feet. They read, "He smells. He cusses. He's aloof." I watched as Daniel drew the words, "A dork" above Oscar's head with an arrow pointing at all of the lines and circles shooting out of Oscar's head. Finally, he dated the page *9-22-93*.

I knew that any child psychologist could see that Daniel's relationship with Oscar was anything but *healthy*. I turned to him,

"Sweetheart, that's a very interesting picture. Is that how you feel about your dad?"

"Yeah, he isn't always nice to me, Nana."

"I know. That's why we're here today. We want him to treat you better and not hurt you anymore." He leaned close to hug me.

Suddenly, Oscar flew out the courtroom door, glared at me and stormed down the hall to the elevator. Crystal, Steve and Steve's attorney came out next.

"I'm dying to know what happened in there, after Oscar's dramatic exit just now."

Crystal grinned. "Judge Groff directed Oscar to begin attending psychological counseling to work on his anger and parenting issues for six months."

Steve added, "During that time, the only way he can visit with Daniel is if the Court Psychologist calls me to bring Daniel to attend their visit."

Steve's attorney shook my hand. "I can't tell you how important your notes were with Judge Groff. He read every page and grilled Oscar on many of the incidents."

Daniel remarked, "Does that mean he can't hit me anymore?"

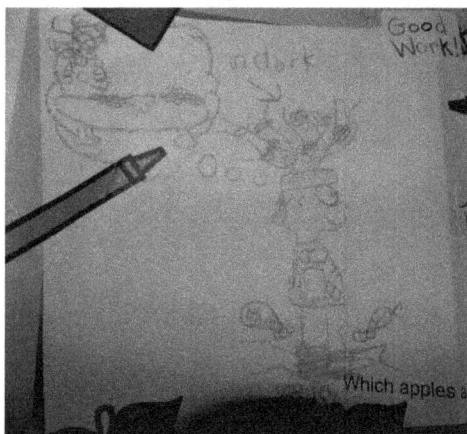

Daniel's Drawing of Oscar the Day of Court

"He was wrong to ever hit you, honey. No more hurts from him. If he does it again, let me, your mom or Steve know about it immediately."

Daniel grinned. "Mom, look at the picture I drew of my dad today."

When he held it up for the three of them to see, I could tell by their expressions that Daniel's drawing spoke volumes. It could have been aptly titled, *Oscar, the Abuser.*

✳ ✳ ✳

I was thrilled for Daniel that Oscar was being forced to address his parenting and anger issues. *Sadly, to this day Crystal has yet to thank me for the many hours I gladly spent to protect my grandson.* Had I not done so, she would have had to hire someone for all of those every-other-weekend visits for the past two years.

✳ ✳ ✳

When I arrived at work the next day, the Union Secretary handed me a letter in the lunchroom. I opened it up. It was a report from the Investigating Committee regarding Lori's charge against me. I read their brief statement.

"We find no Union Law that requires any Union Member to be friends with another Union Member. Case closed."

I looked at the Union Secretary and flashed a quick grin. "There was never a doubt in my mind that I was correct. I pick and choose my own personal friends. Thank you." I stuffed the letter into her hand and went to my work area.

✳ ✳ ✳

On Saturday, I met with Dr. Warner to discuss my book. He surprised me. "I know if I can get your first eight chapters in the hands of the right publisher, they will want your book."

"Which publisher would be the best for me?"

"My problem is that I can't decide what genre to put your book into. It is more like a *Woman in Jeopardy* genre, but there's no such genre like that yet."

"Then, what should I do?"

"For now, I'd like for you to take my screenwriting class."

"Why do I need to do that?"

"Because when I do find you a publisher and they make an offer on your book, if you already have a screenplay about it, they will also buy it for a nice sum of money."

"Then, I'll enroll in your screenwriting class."

✳ ✳ ✳

The next morning, my head was whirring. *Gee, so much to do, so little time; parent, Union President, novelist, divorce attorney and soon to be screenwriter. I think it's time to go dancing and relax.*

And that's what I did. I spent the next five nights dancing at my two favorite C&W places, *Cowboy's Rendezvous* and *Bronco Billy's Bar. The only thing that relaxes me more than dancing is, well you know, a good roll in the hay.*

The following week, I called the Junior College and enrolled in Dr. Warner's screenwriting class on Tuesday nights. When I hung up, Stacy phoned me. "Mom, are you busy right now?"

My chuckle made Stacy curious. "What?"

"Of course, I'm busy, but I'm never too busy for you, honey. What's up?"

"Someone's in town that I want you to meet."

"Who is it?"

"A famous person."

"In your industry?"

"Kind of, yes."

"I don't want to tell you a name. I want you to be surprised."

"Okay, where am I meeting this person?"

"Meet me at *The Granville Inn* on Bluebird Lane in fifteen minutes and bring your camera."

I laughed. "Better make it one hour. I just woke up."

"Sounds good, Mom."

An hour later, I parked and walked into the hotel lobby. Stacy was waiting. I could see he was quite excited. "Mom, this is a very famous person in the industry."

"Male or female?"

"Kind of both."

"That's not possible."

"Sort of an impersonator. You'll see."

We rode the elevator to the seventh floor and went to Room #714. Stacy knocked, and a muscular guy opened the door. "Come on in, Stacy."

"This is my mom. She's here to meet Kitty."

I smiled and shook the young man's hand. "She'll be out in a minute. She's putting on her make-up."

Stacy and I sat in chairs and waited. Ten minutes passed when a six-foot-two woman swept into the room wearing all black, tons of makeup and a gorgeous blonde wig. Stacy stood up. "Kitty La Flame, this is my mom."

I quickly rose. Kitty rushed across the room and grabbed me in a big hug. "Hi, Mom!"

I was instantly mesmerized. "I'm so happy to meet you."

"Kitty is in town to perform at my new club opening tonight."

"Can I go, or is it X-rated?"

Kitty's laugh was boisterous but warm. "Honey, for you, I'll do my best to keep it clean, but I can be a mouthy bitch."

"Mom, the first half of the show is okay for you to see, but not the second half."

"Great, I'll see you tonight, Kitty!"

"Mom, before we go, please take our picture."

I grabbed my camera in my purse and snapped a picture of Stacy and Kitty. Then, she motioned to me. "Stacy, I must have my picture with your lovely Mom. Come over here, Mom!" When I stood beside Kitty, I realized how tall she was. She wrapped her arm around me and exclaimed, "Two blonde bombshells! Wow!"

Stacy took our picture. Kitty kissed my cheek. "See you tonight, doll!"

After Kitty hugged Stacy, we left. On the way down the elevator, I turned to Stacy. "So, I take it that Kitty is a guy?"

"Yes, he's a famous drag-diva, has directed many gay porn films and owns *Grandiose Video.*"

"How does he look when he's a guy?"

"A lot different, no makeup and lots of fun, but he can be quite opinionated on occasion. If you come tonight, be prepared for a raunchy show. That's Kitty's expertise."

"Okay, if it gets too much, I can slip out the door."

"Don't be surprised. It will probably happen."

✳ ✳ ✳

That night, I parked in front of *The Out-Look Club* and went inside to find Stacy. He gave me a quick tour before show time.

I sat behind a rail at the back of the room and watched the famous Kitty La Flame perform. She was spicy, sultry and just right up to the edge of being too much for my ears. When, she spotted me in the back of the room, she waved. "Hi, Mom!"

All heads turned to see me at once. My face flushed, but I managed a wave and smile for Kitty. Stacy was standing to the left of the stage chewing gum and grinning.

After the first half of the show, I found Stacy. "It's time for me to leave. Kitty was extremely raunchy, but oh so funny. Tell her I truly enjoyed her show."

"Glad you came, Mom!"

"What a great opening night for your new club, honey!"

✳ ✳ ✳

Come morning, I went onto Stacy's *Sawyer Stallion Forum* and found several new interesting posts.

From: Nick. "Were your parents supportive of your career choice, or did they want nothing to do with it?"

From: Sawyer. "A picture says a thousand words, and I love to answer this question with a photo of my mother." Below Stacy's reply was my photo with Kitty La Flame. Below the picture he wrote, "Thanks!! Sawyer."

Next, I saw a new comment appear in Sawyer's comment box.

Subject: MOM'S THE WORD! From: Patrick. "Wow, Chris, what a great supportive and loving mother you have! WHAT A LIFE!! We should all be so lucky."

From: Sawyer. "Yes, I am very lucky to have such a supportive mother. I sent her a DVD of my first movie, *but I had my DVD author make it so that it would only play the storyline for her, not any XXX material.* Thanks!! Sawyer."

✳ ✳ ✳

By chance, I ran across a notice in the newspaper for a *Writer's Conference* a few days later. Since I had never attended one, I decided to sign up and buy a ticket to attend.

Two days later, they mailed me an entry blank, if I wanted to enter four chapters of any book I had written into their competition. I was interested. *What the heck!* I sent back the entry blank, four chapters and an entry fee.

✳ ✳ ✳

The following day, my phone rang. "Hi, goodlookin', I'm driving to town with some nice furniture. I thought maybe you or Stacy could use it."

"No, I don't need any furniture. Ask Crystal first and call me back."

"*I already talked to her.* She claims that she has more than enough furniture. What about Stacy?"

"I'll phone him. Call me back in ten minutes."

I dialed Stacy's number. "Hi, honey, Bart's in town with some furniture he needs to get rid of, instead of driving it all the way to Oregon. Would you like to have it?"

"Yeah, I need a good dining room set if he has one."

When Bart called back, I answered. "Stacy's interested in a dining room set."

"Great! I have one that will knock his socks off. Give me his address."

I rattled off Stacy's address for Bart. He jotted it down. "Will you be there, too? I'd like to see you again."

"No, that's not a good idea."

"Okay, talk to you later."

When I drove home from work that night, a truck was parked outside my home. I parked my car, and Bart stepped out of his truck. "Don't be mad. I wanted to see you one more time."

"Well, here I am. Now what?"

"Can I at least kiss you goodbye?"

"No!" I turned to walk inside. He came up behind me on the porch. As I unlocked my front door, he kissed my neck.

"Please don't do that!"

I pushed the front door open. Bart grabbed me with both arms and kissed me. "I'm sorry, baby, I just couldn't help myself."

"Go away and leave me alone. Make a new life in Oregon. We've been over for a long time."

"I know; I screwed up big time."

"It's late. I'm tired. Please leave."

Bart looked at me and cocked his eyebrow to flirt. "Even angry, you're still beautiful!" He turned and left.

I shut the door, locked it and burst into tears. *Damn him and the horse he rode in on!*

✳ ✳ ✳

Crystal, Daniel, Adam Gentry and Kay Marie came by the house one Saturday morning. Daniel had a disk with *Doom* on it that wouldn't work.

"Mom, will you call Stacy to see if he knows how to fix Daniel's disk?"

"Sure thing." *I walked to my phone in amazement. Doom is okay for Daniel, but a Robin Hood movie isn't?*

"Stacy, do you know how to fix a game disk?"

"Sorry Mom, I don't."

Crystal stood up. "Adam Gentry and Kay Marie, it's time to go buy you some new shoes. We'll be back in a while."

After they left, I smiled at Daniel. "Do you know that you are going to move and live with your mom in July?"

"Yes, I know."

"How do you feel about it?"

"Sad."

"Every time Mom calls Steve, he calls all of us together and has the other kids crying. Steve calls my mom irresponsible for going out late at night."

"Honey, if Steve is making you, your brothers and sister cry, he is being irresponsible."

When Crystal returned to pick Daniel up, I told her what Daniel said about what Steve was doing to the kids when she calls.

After Daniel left with Crystal and the other two kids, she drove them to Steve's and asked him about Daniel's comments.

Later, she phoned me. "Steve claims Daniel isn't telling the truth."

"Really? Just remember that Steve asked me to lie to you and I refused. He has a pattern of doing this."

"Betty said that Daniel might start lying to keep us together."

Four days later, Crystal called me at work. *"Daniel told me you hate Steve."*

"Why don't you bring him by early this Sunday, so the three of us can talk? It's time for Daniel to be confronted by me."

✳ ✳ ✳

That Sunday morning, the three of us sat down in my den for a talk. I smiled at Daniel. "Honey, your mom tells me that you believe I hate Steve. Is that correct?"

Daniel couldn't look me in the eye. "I don't know."

"Who knows if you don't?"

He shrugged his shoulders.

"We understand how upset you are that your mom and Steve are getting a divorce, but making up stories isn't going to change anything. It will only make things more difficult."

A few tears rolled from the corner of Daniel's eyes.

"If Nana didn't love you, I wouldn't care if you made up stories that aren't true. But I do love you. We all do. Honey, it isn't okay to tell a lie. It only hurts others and makes things worse. Can you understand what I'm saying?"

Daniel dropped head. "Yes, I do. I understand."

"That's good, so from now on, no more making up stories, because you are upset over what is going on at home. Okay?"

He bit his lip and nodded. "Okay."

I gave him a big hug. "I'll always love you, sweetheart."

As I walked them to the front door, I stopped. "Daniel, do you like your new school, now that you're living with your Mom?"

He looked at Crystal and ducked his head. "Crystal, is he living with you or not?"

"I don't want to talk about it. We have to go."

✳ ✳ ✳

As luck would have it, it was my day to see Betty the next day. After I updated her on my past two weeks, an unexpected visit from Bart and my recent Daniel drama, Betty sighed. "It is time for you to also own *your own reality*. For almost two years, I have done everything I could think of to get this man out of your head and your heart."

I bit my lip and dropped my head. I knew that Betty was at her wit's end with me over my continued feelings for Bart.

"There is only one thing left for me to try. I want you to leave here today and buy a book called *People of the Lie* by Scott M. Peck. If his book can't reach you, no one can. Debbie, there are some people in this world who *can't be helped, because they have a hole in their soul. They have no conscience."*

"I know, Betty. I've tried so hard to get him out of my mind." Tears rolled down my cheeks.

She handed me her box of Kleenex. "Take it. You need it worse than I do. That man is a psychopath."

After I drove away from her building that day, I went straight to a bookstore and purchased *People of the Lie.*

When I arrived home from work that evening, I opened my computer and read an overview of the book on Barnes & Noble's webpage. The words, "disturbing, fascinating and impossible to put down," stood out, *but am I ready to take a journey into the examination of human evil, as it relates directly to Bart?*

22

≈

To Sink or Heal

With Dr. Scott M. Peck's book in hand, I walked into my bedroom, turned on a bright light and began to read *People of the Lie*. I found it to be *disturbing* at first. Likely, it's because I mentally fought against believing that Bart could indeed be one of those evil people. After all, he was so charming, likeable and lovable to me when I first met him.

The more I read, *the more fascinated I became* to think that these charming, likeable and lovable people aren't real. They are human façades wearing false curtains that allow them to conceal their true self and exist in our world with zero ability to feel any empathy for the pain and havoc they eagerly create in the lives of others; i.e., *no conscience within, no feelings onboard.*

Halfway through the book, I began to sense something changing within me. It was as if my rose-colored glasses were slowly melting away to the point that I could no longer deny to myself that Dr. Peck was, in fact, precisely diagnosing my problem with Bart, even though I had never met him. With each turn of a page, I weaved back-and-forth in my attempts to dodge his truth bullets. I secretly hoped to uncover one flaw in his brilliant probe into the *Mechanics of Evil* and disprove his many years of patient observation and evaluation. None were found.

I slowly began to yield to the stark reality that Dr. Peck was speaking directly to me and also to my heart, when he pointed out that the healing of human evil must start within us. My quandary was *the how of it.* Say that I could learn to see through people with no conscience to protect myself. How does my awakening help heal human evil in the world?

After finishing his book, I wrote an honest list of what I believed to be Bart's worst traits. Narcissistic, deceptive liar, twisted motives, control over others, bored with good people and established fear in others. I realized Bart's treatment of me and others sounded exactly like a kind of evil.

He used and misused family, friends, neighbors and co-workers for his own selfish enjoyment and gain. He felt *nothing* when lives were destroyed, hearts were broken and banks were burglarized to feed his bottomless greed. He left a *Trail of Misery* behind him that he wore like a badge of egotistical honor to himself. *For self is all that matters to Bart.*

I finally woke up to the fact that Bart delighted in the sorrow and pain of others, for they were the only source that could feed his insatiable hunger for the thrill of power and ravenous narcissism. His *Emptiness of Soul* was the engine that drove him to constantly stalk innocent victims. For without destroying others, he felt dangerously empty within and without.

My answer of how to heal human evil rose out of my constant soul-searching. I found it after I had finished reading *People of the Lie.* By healing my mind and senses to recognize anyone I meet who would victimize me, or another person, and possessed no conscience and had *a hole in their soul,* I could then learn to protect myself and also assist other victims to do likewise. *I will no longer allow anyone to kill my spirit to control me, including those who are sick with jealousy or the love of power, be it friend, foe or family. Nor will I be fodder for their starving emptiness and grandiosity to feed their empty soul.*

✻ ✻ ✻

The Writer's Conference was the next day. When I arrived, I discovered that the conference was actually for Romance Writers. That wasn't my genre for sure, but I enjoyed the conference anyway. That afternoon, I picked out a class to attend that had a visiting New York Editor looking for new material. I was impressed with his presentation and the fact that his publisher was only looking for *cutting-edge material.* I believed that my book, then titled *Daddy's Girl,* fit perfectly within that description.

After class ended, I eagerly awaited my chance to pitch my book to the blonde-headed editor. As I finished my short pitch, I knew he was interested, when he handed me his card.

"Have your agent contact me."

"I will for sure." I left the conference on *Cloud Nine.*

When I returned home, I phoned Dr. Warner, gave him the editor's information and requested that he mail the first six chapters of my book to the editor.

✻ ✻ ✻

Three weeks later on a Sunday morning, I stepped outside my front door and retrieved my newspaper. When I got to the Theater Section, I turned a page. A large headline caught my eye. *Best Theatrical Marketing Tool; Cast a Porn Star in Your Holocaust Drama.*

I wonder who that Porn Star could be.

As I read the story, I discovered my answer. "Last night, local porn star, Sawyer Stallion, star of international gay video hits, spent a good ten minutes strolling the stage buck naked before his throat was cut by a Nazi officer in the play. Accurately, Sawyer had more tan lines than stage lines."

I waited until I thought Stacy would be awake to call him. "Hi honey, you got quite a write up in today's newspaper."

"What page is it on? I want to read it."

"Page Three of the Theater Section. You didn't mention anything to me about doing a play."

"I was afraid to, Mom. I knew you'd want to come, and I couldn't go onstage with you in the audience."

That made me laugh. "Thank you, honey."

"Mom, I have more news."

"What's that?"

"I have a boyfriend named Preston Griffin."

"When do I get to meet Preston?"

"He spent the night with me. How about we take you to lunch?"

"Deal! Where shall I meet you and Preston?"

"I know you love seafood. How about we meet you at Zider Zee's in an hour?"

"I'll be there."

Stacy and Preston were waiting in the lobby, when I arrived. Preston was courteous and good-looking. After we were seated, Stacy seemed edgy. "Preston does the same thing that I do, Mom."

"Oh, you manage a bar, too?"

"No, Ma'am, I'm a *Porn Star* like Stacy."

Stacy grinned. "Preston and I are about to star in a new porn video together called *The Twins*."

"Well, you both have dark hair, and you're very attractive, but Preston isn't quite as tall."

"It's only porn, Mom, not a big movie production."

I laughed. "True. So Preston, what's your porn name?"

"I am Dakota Blaze."

"That's a good name for porn."

As I drove away that day, I was happy for Stacy that he had found a boyfriend and seemed so happy.

✳ ✳ ✳

Two weeks later, I drove downtown to the Red Rock County Court building. It was divorce day number four, only this time, I was my own attorney. I entered Judge Crawford's Courtroom before anyone else, except the Court Bailiff. I took a seat near the front; my papers were drawn up and ready to go.

The room filled up before Judge Crawford entered the Courtroom. The Court Bailiff called my name out first to approach. Judge Crawford was a female. "Mrs. Debbie Austin, are you ready?"

I stood up and approached the bench. "I am, Your Honor." I handed her my papers. She looked them over with a scowl. "You can't be your own attorney, Mrs. Austin. I deal with lots of people like you all day long. You'll be back in here at least six more times, because you forgot to cover something in your agreement. You need to go find a *real attorney.*"

"No, Ma'am, I've covered everything. There is absolutely no problem with my paperwork."

She frowned and handed me my papers. "They weren't date stamped. Go down the hall."

"No one told me they needed to be date stamped."

"Go get them stamped."

"Okay." I turned and walked to the Court Bailiff. He directed me down her back hallway to a Court Secretary. She put a date stamp on my papers and handed them back to me. "That's it?"

"That's it."

"I arrived first today. You all need to put up a sign, if this date stamp is that important people need to know it must be done first."

She just shrugged. I turned, re-entered Judge Crawford's Courtroom and sat down. Rather than placing my papers on top of the Wait List, the Court Bailiff placed them on the *bottom* of the stack. I was almost the last person to stand before Judge Crawford later that day. She merely signed my papers and stated, "You're done."

✳ ✳ ✳

When I got home, I phoned Mother. "Hi Momma, good news, I'm now a divorced woman again."

"Why didn't you just get your marriage annulled?"

"Mother, it doesn't work that way. We did consummate our marriage."

"So what name are you going to go by now?"

"I've been married to two different men with the last name Austin, so I'm still Debbie Austin."

"You should change it!"

"Seriously? To what, Tim's last name, Jack's last name, or how about my dad's last name?"

"Oh, forget it. Austin is better than any of those names."

"Thank you, Mother."

I hung up. *Enough of her negativity.*

✳ ✳ ✳

I didn't like how that call went, so I hoped Crystal would be more positive. "Hi Honey, I'm a free woman again."

"Can you keep Daniel this weekend, Mom?"

"I'd love to. I want to take him to Wet & Wild. We'll have lots of fun there."

"No, you can't take him to Wet & Wild."

"Why not?"

"Because I decide where he can go, not you."

"First, you ask me to keep him, and then you want to argue with me about taking him to Wet & Wild. Are you still going to that crazy church?"

"No."

"Then, what's the problem with Wet & Wild? You and I have gone there many times together."

"Oh, forget it. Just come pick him up. I have plans."

"I'm on my way."

✳ ✳ ✳

Daniel and I had a blast at Wet & Wild. We didn't miss doing one thing in that whole waterpark. We swam in the big motion pool, rode inner tubes around the park, came down the giant water slide too many times to count, and at the end of the day, we were both a bit sunburned. On the way home, I drove through *Burger Street* to get us some food and drinks. After we got home and ate, Daniel crashed on the couch. The next day, I drove him to Crystal's apartment.

The following weekend, I called Steve. "Hi, can I pick up Wayne, Adam Gentry and Kay Marie this weekend for a visit?"

"You know you can. They've been missing you."

When I rang Steve's doorbell, he stepped outside and closed the door. "The kids don't know it yet, but I'm getting married again next month."

"Congratulations! Who's the lucky lady?"

"Dorothy Blake. We met at our church."

"I'm sure the kids will be thrilled to death, but I won't say a word about it."

Steve opened his door. "Nana's here, time for your visit."

All three kids raced out the door to my Firebird. They always scuffled to see who would sit in my front seat, so I set up a system for it. "Whose turn is the front seat today?"

Adam jumped into the seat. "Mine, Nana! Kay Marie rode up here last time." I nodded, made sure everyone was wearing their seatbelt and took off to see a movie. On the way I put in my latest funny, Bob Rivers CD. The kids and I always sang along. Adam always knew every word to each song the best. He was also the joker of the group. He kept us laughing the whole way there.

We agreed to go see *Jurassic Park.* I bought them popcorn and drinks, and we headed inside to see the movie. When the movie started, silly Adam let out a loud dinosaur roar.

After the movie, we stopped at *Good Eats* for a meal. I didn't know which of the three kids was the funniest. We laughed, made funny faces, and they colored pictures with weird messages for me.

On the way to Steve's, I turned on my funny song CD again. Adam began to adlib new words to the songs that were even funnier than the ones Bob Rivers wrote.

After I parked, they raced to see who could get to their front door first. I followed them. Steve invited me inside and showed me some great studio pictures that he had made of the kids.

Time to leave soon arrived. I hugged and tickled each one of them before I left.

Life is good! My family is finally on the mend, thanks in great part to Betty T.

23

≈

Say It Isn't So

It was time for my 69th visit with Betty. When I arrived, she seemed especially happy. I updated her on my past two weeks and told her that I read Scott M. Peck's book. She asked about my reactions to his message describing truly evil people who have *no conscience and want to harm others.*

I smiled. "Betty, the book worked. I can't explain it, but Dr. Peck finally got it through my thick head. Not at first, but further into his book. I began to see the real Bart and how he hurts other people, with no thought of the pain he causes."

"What did you feel when you finished his book?"

"It was as if I just awoke from a long sleep, and I'm no longer under the spell of a *Snake Charmer.*"

"Debbie, you have finally made it through the dark forest and are standing safely on the other side, just as I had promised you. Congratulations, you made it!"

I couldn't help but beam over her compliment.

She handed me an envelope. "I know you've been writing *Daddy's Girl.*"

"What's in this envelope?"

She grinned. "Open it and see."

Betty had written an epilogue for *Daddy's Girl*. Here is what she wrote and gave to me that day.

✳ ✳ ✳

"Debbie Austin survived, but she not only survived, she has now created a life full of energy, hope and purpose."

"Not all addicts are so fortunate. Many do not survive. Some commit suicide, and some live in a blur of fantasy and addiction. Others just exist to walk painfully through *quiet lives of desperation* with no understanding of *why.*"

"Abuse is generational. Just as little children are taught to be mannerly, trusting, optimistic, and kind by watching the examples set by those in charge of their upbringing, they also emulate other traits of their caregivers such as hopelessness, anger, insensitivity and abuse to others. Children absorb the good and bad attributes of their elders, and then they *become their learned experiences.* Sadly, that means that more victims and abusers are born generationally."

In Debbie's case, she lived out her parent's example. Her life was composed of abusers and victims. She played the victim role she had learned so well from her mother and from her own victimization at the hands of her father. Time and time again, she repeated her learned pattern."

"Consequently, her children, Crystal and Stacy, were sucked into the same dysfunctional cycle by experiencing a world inhabited by immature parents who were self-involved and did not protect children from adult sexuality. And so, Debbie's children were doomed to live out the old generational pain passed down from her parents and grandparents, and they would then pass it on to their children."

"Somewhere along the way, Debbie found the courage to step forward and demand a new way of living. Fortunately for Crystal and Stacy, Debbie's courage can become generational, for as of this writing; Stacy has demonstrated the courage to break the *chain of dysfunction* by becoming involved in a recovery effort of his own. There is now hope, that if he continues that recovery, his life will be enriched beyond his wildest dreams. That is my greatest wish for him."

"The prison of generational abuse can only be escaped through hard work on the part of all concerned. In time, I hope that Crystal will continue to deal with her demons and do more in-depth counseling. *Otherwise, she will continue the painful role of victim and/or abuser.* If she never walks through the same dark forest to do the hard work that her mother and brother, Stacy, have done, her life will continue to be filled with unhappiness and broken relationships. *For no healing can surface for her or her children, until she finds that willingness and takes full responsibility for her own actions and forges a new life for her generational family line.* Otherwise, her addictive behavior of *victim and abuser* will never cease to be continually perpetuated in her generational family."

"And so, Debbie's story will not end here, for there's hope that *both of her children will, in time, walk in her footsteps.*"

The letter was signed; "Betty T., M.Ed., LPC, Psychotherapist, November 16, 1993."

✹ ✹ ✹

I was speechless for a moment. "Thank you, Betty, for taking the time to write such a touching epilogue for my book. Your wish and pathway for my children's healing and happiness is my greatest prayer."

She smiled. "Now it's time for congratulations! You have made a long, difficult journey and done amazing, though gut-wrenching work. You no longer need me. This is our last visit."

My chin dropped. I shook my head. "I don't think I can make it without you, Betty."

"Yes, you can. I'm always here if things should change, but you have grown so much since we first began. I have faith in you to pick up your life and continue forward without my help."

She stood up and reached out her arms. "Give me one more hug." I did it, but it wasn't without flowing tears, and then, I left her office. *Can I truly make it all by myself now? I must believe, for I am no longer that helpless victim who walked into Betty T.'s office many months ago, and it feels wonderful!*

✳ ✳ ✳

It didn't take but a few weeks, before I had to face my first challenge alone without Betty's guidance.

I phoned Stacy. "Honey, I want to take you to lunch and tell you my news."

"Sure Mom. What time?"

"I'll pick you up in thirty minutes."

When I parked outside Stacy's condo, I only waited a few minutes before he opened his second-story door. He was wearing shorts and a tank top. I was stunned at how huge his arms and legs had become. Then, he opened my car door and sat down.

"Would you believe Betty cut me loose a few weeks ago?"

"Wow, that's great news!"

As I drove us toward a busy intersection on the way to our favorite Mexican restaurant, there was no red light at the busy intersection. I waited and waited. Not one driver would pause and leave room to allow me to cross to the other lane and turn left.

Suddenly, Stacy jumped out of my car, stormed in front of several moving cars and began to scream at the drivers. "Stop your damn cars! Let us cross the fucking street!"

I was stunned and afraid an angry driver might jump out with a gun and shoot him right there in front of me. The incident left me trembling in fear that I could suddenly lose my son at any moment.

Plus, I had *never* seen him behave like that in my life. The incident totally overwhelmed me.

After we ate, I dropped him off at his condo and returned home. I called one of my dance partners and described Stacy's muscles and his explosive reaction earlier.

"Debbie, does your son take steroids?"

"Not that I know of, why do you ask?"

"Have you ever heard of Roid Rages?"

"What are Roid Rages?"

End of Book Two

✶✶✶

This is a Four Book Series